THE
INCOMPETENT
SPECIALIST

THE
INCOMPETENT
SPECIALIST

How to Evaluate, Document Performance, and Dismiss School Staff

C. Edward Lawrence
Myra K. Vachon

CORWIN PRESS, INC.
A Sage Publications Company
Thousand Oaks, California

For information address:

 Corwin Press, Inc.
A Sage Publications Company
2455 Teller Road
Thousand Oaks, California 91320
E-mail: order@corwin.sagepub.com

SAGE Publications Ltd.
6 Bonhill Street
London EC2A 4PU
United Kingdom

SAGE Publications India Pvt. Ltd.
M-32 Market
Greater Kailash I
New Delhi 110 048 India

Printed in the United States of America

Library of Congress Cataloging-in-Publication Data

Lawrence, C. Edward.
    The incompetent specialist: How to evaluate, document
performance, and dismiss school staff / authors, C. Edward Lawrence,
Myra K. Vachon.
        p.   cm.
    Includes bibliographical references and index.
    ISBN 0-8039-6439-0 (pbk.: acid-free paper).—ISBN 0-8039-6438-2
(cloth : acid-free paper)
        1. Special education teachers—Rating of—United States.
    2. Special education teachers—Dismissal of—United States.
    I. Vachon, Myra K.   II. Title.
    LB2838.L28   1996
    371.1'44—dc20   96-25204

This book is printed on acid-free paper.

97 98 99 00 01 02 10 9 8 7 6 5 4 3 2 1

Acquiring Editor: Gracia Alkema
Editorial Assistant: Nicole Fountain
Production Editor: Astrid Virding
Production Assistant: Sherrise Purdum
Typesetter & Designer: Andrea D. Swanson
Cover Designer: Marcia R. Finlayson

Contents

List of Sample Documents

(Although some documents may be used more than once, they are listed only under the heading of the first chapter in which they are introduced.)

CORWIN
PRESS

A Cautionary Note

This guide book on the implementation of an evaluation process that meets just-cause requirements and follows due process procedures is not a legal document. Rather, it is intended to provide accurate information about the subject matter, and it is sold with the understanding that the publisher and the authors are not engaged in rendering legal advice or other professional services. Specifically, the recommendations contained herein are guidelines only—not legal advice. Moreover, the publisher and the authors do not warrant, in any manner, suitability of these guidelines for any particular usage. If you require legal advice or other expert assistance, contact an attorney or other competent legal professional who has knowledge of all laws pertaining to your situation and the jurisdiction prevailing for your school district.

Preface

This guide evolved through the experiences of the authors and through input from colleagues, school administrators and supervisors participating in workshops, in-service classes, and university graduate courses. At these workshops and classes we found that, although most school administrators had taken a law class that covered general legal issues, they had received little practical information about how to conduct staff evaluations, especially on procedures to dismiss incompetent specialists, particularly those specialists working with children who have special needs (e.g., guidance counselors, psychologists, social workers, speech clinicians, physical therapists, occupational therapists).

School administrators and supervisors must become familiar with state and federal laws, rules, and regulations as well as the policies and procedures of the school district with regard to implementation of Public Law 94-142. The purpose of this law is to protect and improve the quality of education for children who have special needs. This law is not designed to protect incompetent specialists or teachers working with special-needs children. Nevertheless, its implementation can inadvertently be used by some specialists, teachers, or both to fend off an unsatisfactory evaluation. Special-needs children require the services of competent specialists, and the needs of these children must be placed before the needs of the incompetent specialist. This book explains the procedures used to document and evaluate the work of the incompetent school specialist to recommend his or her dismissal.

We thank Robert Hanson, all school administrators, supervisors, and colleagues who provided suggestions and comments that were vital to the completion of this guide. Finally, we acknowledge the support, encouragement, and editorial assistance provided by Gracia Alkema and the staff at Corwin Press.

C. Edward Lawrence
Myra K. Vachon

About the Authors

C. Edward Lawrence is Assistant Superintendent of Leadership and Support Services for the Milwaukee School District in Milwaukee, Wisconsin, where he has had an extensive career in various educational roles. He has served as a teacher; counselor; team leader and assistant principal at the elementary, middle, and high school levels; elementary and middle school principal; director of alternative programs; and community superintendent. He has been a hearing officer for unsatisfactory teacher evaluations, second-step misconduct cases, and immediate suspensions of staff. In addition, he has conducted workshops for school administrators on how to prepare for and win unsatisfactory teacher evaluation and misconduct cases. He holds a Ph.D. degree in urban education from the University of Wisconsin-Milwaukee, where he is an adjunct instructor in the Department of Administrative Leadership, teaching courses in instructional supervision and school personnel as well as critical issues in education, including supervision of incompetent and marginal teachers. He is coauthor (with Myra K. Vachon, D. O. Leake, & B. H. Leake) of *The Marginal Teacher: A Step-by-Step Guide to Fair Identification and Dismissal* (1993). His most recent publication (with Myra K. Vachon) is *How to Handle Staff Misconduct: A Step-by-Step Guide* (1995).

Myra K. Vachon is Director of Staffing Services for the Milwaukee School District in Milwaukee, Wisconsin. During her career in the Milwaukee School District, she has served as a teacher, department chairwoman, curriculum and instruction supervisor, school administrator, assistant to the community superintendent, and leadership specialist. She has supervised preservice and in-service classroom teachers, served as a hearing officer for unsatisfactory teacher evaluations and second-step misconduct cases, advised principals with regard to teacher supervisory procedures and techniques, and conducted workshops for school administrators on how to prepare for and win unsatisfactory teacher evaluations and misconduct cases. She has served as an adjunct instructor in the Education Department at Alverno College teaching science methods courses for elementary teachers. She holds a Ph.D. in urban education from the University of Wisconsin-Milwaukee, where she has taught courses in the Department of Administrative Leadership on supervising instructional staff and critical issues in education. She is coauthor (with C. Edward Lawrence, D. O. Leake, & B. H. Leake) of *The Marginal Teacher: A Step-by-Step Guide to Fair Identification and Dismissal* (1993). Her most recent publication (with C. Edward Lawrence) is *How to Handle Staff Misconduct: A Step-by-Step Guide* (1995).

Introduction

For school administrators, conducting performance evaluations is a major responsibility. Still, a large number of administrators are reluctant to evaluate school specialists, teachers who work with students who have special needs, or both. Students in special education classes have needs that must be addressed by their classroom teachers as well as by nonclassroom professionals. In this guide, the term *specialist* encompasses a variety of nonclassroom staff members (e.g., guidance counselors, social workers, school psychologists, speech clinicians, physical therapists, occupational therapists). This guide focuses primarily on personnel who serve in special roles; however, procedures can be adapted to cases involving teachers in special education classes for children who are severely physically handicapped, autistic, mentally handicapped, learning handicapped, learning disabled, severely emotionally disturbed, visually impaired, or hearing impaired.

Most school administrators are former general education classroom teachers. Consequently, they are usually more comfortable evaluating the performance of general education teachers, regardless of their own past teaching experience or area of certification, than they are evaluating specialists and special education teachers. Moreover, school administrators frequently state that they are unprepared to properly supervise and evaluate school specialists or teachers working in special education. In fact, some school administrators admit that they lack training on how to effectively handle performance problems that could eventually result in the dismissal of specialists. Some excuses that administrators may use to avoid difficult evaluations, those that may lead to dismissal, are that such evaluations are time consuming, are often overturned by an arbitrator, and usually do not improve the specialist's or teacher's performance. Because of the small number of special education children in a school and the small number of specialists working with them compared with the total school population, many administrators ignore the difficult task of evaluating incompetent specialists. Some administrators and supervisors will make staff adjustments to avoid facing up to the specialist's incompetence. The administrator may change the specialist's duties, ask another staff member to work with the specialist, or simply close his or her eyes and ears hoping that the specialist will transfer to another school.

The task of dismissing a school specialist is probably more difficult than the task of dismissing a regular classroom teacher. In either case, the dismissal process requires a great deal of time and extensive documentation, especially for tenured staff members. Therefore, evaluation procedures that are implemented must ensure that incompetent school specialists are dismissed from the profession before they are granted tenure.

Although it is likely that 99% of all specialists or teachers should be commended for providing excellent services to the school district's special-needs children, it is unfortunate that even 1% of these specialists or special education teachers may be incompetent and hide their incompetence behind Public Law 94-142. These specialists may disguise their incompetence by telling the school administrator or their supervisor that they work with each child on a one-to-one basis or in small groups in their offices and that the administrator's presence will breach the confidentiality of the child and his or her parents. Despite these excuses, the school administrator and supervisor must conduct observations of the specialist, and also be alert to complaints from parents, children, and other staff members about the specialist. Even though the school administrator has clear concerns about the quality of the job that the specialist is performing, the administrator may be in a quandary relative to performance expectations and criteria as well as how to conduct observations and collect documentation.

Even more frustrating for the school administrator is the fact that the work of the specialists frequently includes home visits and other off-site activities that the school administrator cannot observe directly. In addition, the specialists may work at two or more schools. Thus, school administrators may be reluctant to spend too much time evaluating specialists who may work at their school only 1 or 2 days per week. In some cases, the school administrator may coevaluate the specialist with an administrator in another school or with a supervisor from the district office. This sort of situation has inherent problems because of the differences in perception and the amount of time that each evaluator actually spends observing the various facets of the specialist's performance.

Of course, evaluation of any staff member calls for adherence to just-cause requirements and due process, even though a school administrator must use different approaches when evaluating the performance of specialists than when evaluating the performance of classroom teachers. These approaches will be explored throughout this guide. In all cases, you must determine whether specialists are fulfilling their duties and responsibilities at an acceptable level of performance.

So, as the school administrator, you are probably asking, "How can I assist specialists whose performance is unsatisfactory? How can I make the difficult decision to recommend the dismissal of these unsatisfactory specialists?" To assist you, the step-by-step dismissal process presented in this guide is predicated on the following assumptions:

- The purpose of supervision and evaluation is to improve job performance.
- All students, including those with special needs, have an inalienable right to quality education.
- Just cause is required when a recommendation for dismissal is made.
- Due process is required to provide the staff member with an opportunity to hear testimony against him- or herself and an opportunity to respond.

By following the procedures outlined in this guide, you can proceed with the assurance that you have met the due process requirements and that you have provided ample opportunity for either the nontenured or tenured school specialist to improve to meet a satisfactory level of job performance. Each chapter provides suggested protocols, sample forms, sample letters, and administrative tips to facilitate the process to improve job performance of specialists. But, if the performance of the specialist does not improve, be sure that the documentation you have collected can withstand scrutiny at the various steps in the evaluation process.

One key aspect of the evaluation process outlined in this guide is coevaluation of the specialist by the principal and specialist's supervisor. Involvement of the supervisor provides expertise in the specialist's area of service. In any coevaluation arrangement, it is important that both evaluators are consistent in implementing the evaluation procedures. Because principals are usually the official evaluators of staff members in their schools, they should take the lead in the evaluation process during the coevaluation relative to coordinating activities, organizing the documentation, and presenting or presiding at unsatisfactory evaluation conferences and hearings.

Resource A consists of a schematic view showing the relationship among the specialist's evaluators and the evaluators' responsibilities as well as a calendar with a suggested timeline of their actions. A sample unsatisfactory specialist evaluation binder, provided in Resource B, was developed using a guidance counselor as an example of the incompetent specialist. Nevertheless, these procedures, letters, and documents can be easily adapted to cases involving any type of specialist (e.g., social worker, school psychologist, speech clinician, physical therapist, occupational therapist, teacher of special needs students).

How to Use This Guide

This guide does not replace advisement and consultation available to you within your school district. Nevertheless, it does present basic directions and cautions to ensure due process during the evaluation of school specialists and, if necessary, dismissal procedures. If you receive advice from your supervisor, attorney for the school district, or personnel director that is contrary to information in this publication, you should follow that advice.

1

Overview of the Evaluation Process

Remember that personnel matters are confidential.

The purpose of evaluation is to achieve and maintain high standards of job performance for all employees. In the school environment, the evaluation process should (a) improve the quality of educational programs and enhance student learning, (b) provide a vehicle for holding staff accountable for their own performance, (c) aid in the staff selection process for filling other positions, and (d) provide information relative to professional development that is needed (Iwanicki, 1990, p. 159). These apply to all staff members in your school, including those who are in specialist positions.

First, the quality of the specialists that work in your school has a direct impact on the quality of the instructional program. Therefore, the time you devote to evaluating your school specialists will support your efforts in implementing an instructional program that allows all students to reach their highest potential and allows all staff members to work in a safe and secure learning environment. Effective daily operations of the school are essential to providing an educationally stimulating environment for students to learn, staff to teach, and specialists to perform their duties.

The second purpose of evaluation is the accountability that will ensure that only the best specialists continue in their roles. As the school administrator, you are aware that students, parents, other teachers, and the general public are constantly assessing the effectiveness of the specialists (Natriello, 1990, p. 35).

Despite that fact, you must supervise and conduct evaluations of specialists in accordance with state statutes, board policies, and the master contract.

The third purpose of evaluation is to foster the professional development of the specialists. You must provide assistance to specialists as well as to teaching staff. In the case of a specialist whose performance is questionable, a plan for intensive assistance may be necessary to raise his or her performance to an acceptable level. If improvement does not occur, you will need to give the incompetent specialist an opportunity to resign voluntarily.

The fourth purpose of evaluation is to provide information that will aid in the selection and hiring of the best possible specialist. To reduce the efforts you will have to expend dealing with marginal or incompetent staff members, the district personnel office must be vigilant and must hire only the most qualified people.

Finally, the unspoken purpose of evaluation is to dismiss incompetent specialists who cannot perform their duties, or who will not perform their duties at a satisfactory level. To accomplish this, you must prove that the specialist exhibits incompetence on a daily basis, that the specialist was given an opportunity to improve, that you provided support to the specialist, and that the specialist failed to improve. As a result, the specialist should be recommended for dismissal from the school district.

As the coevaluator of the specialist, you must also understand the difference between evaluation and misconduct. As stated above, the objective of evaluation is to assess the staff member's job performance and to clarify expectations for maintaining a satisfactory level of performance. On the other hand, misconduct is the inappropriate conduct of a staff member at school or in the community. For example, misconduct may be an incident or series of incidents involving sexually related conduct; possession of controlled substances; theft and fraud; illegal conduct away from school; use of corporal punishment at school; insubordination; neglect of duty, tardiness, or both. Disposition of misconduct charges may range from warnings to oral or written reprimands to suspension without pay or a recommendation for dismissal (Lawrence & Vachon, 1995, p. 5). Therefore, it is essential that you clearly know the provisions in the master contract relative to evaluation and misconduct. In fact, you must adhere to the provisions of the master contract or you may lose the unsatisfactory evaluation case. Even if your Board of Education upholds your case, an arbitrator or the civil court is likely to overturn it later. As a result, the school district will have to reinstate the individual, and it will also have to pay attorney fees, back wages, and monies for pain and suffering as well as other unexpected expenses.

Like other evaluators, you will be disheartened when you lose your case because you inadvertently violated the master contract. Nevertheless, rumors about the unsatisfactory evaluation may spread to other employees throughout the school district. In fact, the case may become a folktale that will be told over and over to school administrators and supervisors. To avoid this unfortunate defeat, you must follow the procedures in this guide and the steps outlined in the Schematic View of the Steps in the Evaluation Process (see Sample Document 1.1).

Even though some variations naturally occur in the evaluation process used in different school districts and in different schools, you should follow the basic steps that are consistent with due process. Those steps in the evaluation of specialists include the following:

Step 1. Orient all staff members to the evaluation process within the first 30 days of school. This could occur at a regular staff meeting, through information printed in the staff handbook, via a separate memorandum to staff, or all three.

Step 2. Provide a written explanation of the evaluation process, and attach samples of the evaluation instruments and a copy of the evaluation section of the specialist's master contract. Be the sole evaluator of general education teachers and a coevaluator (with their supervisors who have expertise in the specific area) of all school specialists .

Step 3. When conducting planning conferences with general education teachers and specialists, use appropriate forms that are aligned with district expectations and their job descriptions.

Step 4. Conduct observations of all staff members.

Step 5. Collect data from a variety of sources to evaluate the specialists (e.g., observations, complaints from colleagues, parents and students, and other sources).

Step 6. Hold feedback sessions with specialists within 5 school days after the observations, and follow up with a written summary or memorandum of concerns.

Step 7. Implement an intensive assistance plan, if necessary.

Step 8. Make a decision to (a) return the specialist to Step Four of the evaluation process, use summary letters, and memoranda of concerns, develop a plan for intensive assistance; (b) reassign the specialist; or (c) dismiss the specialist.

Step 9. Follow the dismissal procedures as outlined in the master contract, judiciary system, or both.

Step 10. Understand that the dismissal process may take one or more years to resolve.

Administrative Tips to Remember

- ❑ Review board policy on performance standards for school specialists.
- ❑ When handling staff misconduct, adhere to due process requirements and follow contractual procedures.
- ❑ When conducting all performance evaluations, adhere to due process requirements and follow contractual procedures.
- ❑ Develop and implement evaluation procedures that are consistent with district procedures for all school specialists .

❑   Review the job descriptions and requirements for all school specialist positions.

❑   Make sure that each specialist has a copy of his or her most recent job description.

❑   Use the school district's evaluation form to evaluate school specialists.

❑   Base your evaluation on a several observations, not on a single incident.

❑   Base the unsatisfactory evaluation on poor performance rather than on personality differences.

❑   Make sure that each specialist receives a written explanation of the evaluation process.

❑   Provide clear, concise documentation.

❑   Do not include references to the employee's gender, ethnicity, physical handicap, or national origin during the evaluation process.

❑   Keep all evaluation records private, between you and the employee and others who have a right to see them.

❑   Always base your evaluations on specific, written, and clearly communicated job requirements.

❑   Know procedures and have necessary quick references close at hand (written as well as professional advisement).

❑   Allow the employee to see the evaluation and to appeal it if he or she thinks it is unfair.

Sample Document 1.1
Schematic View of the Steps of the Evaluation Process

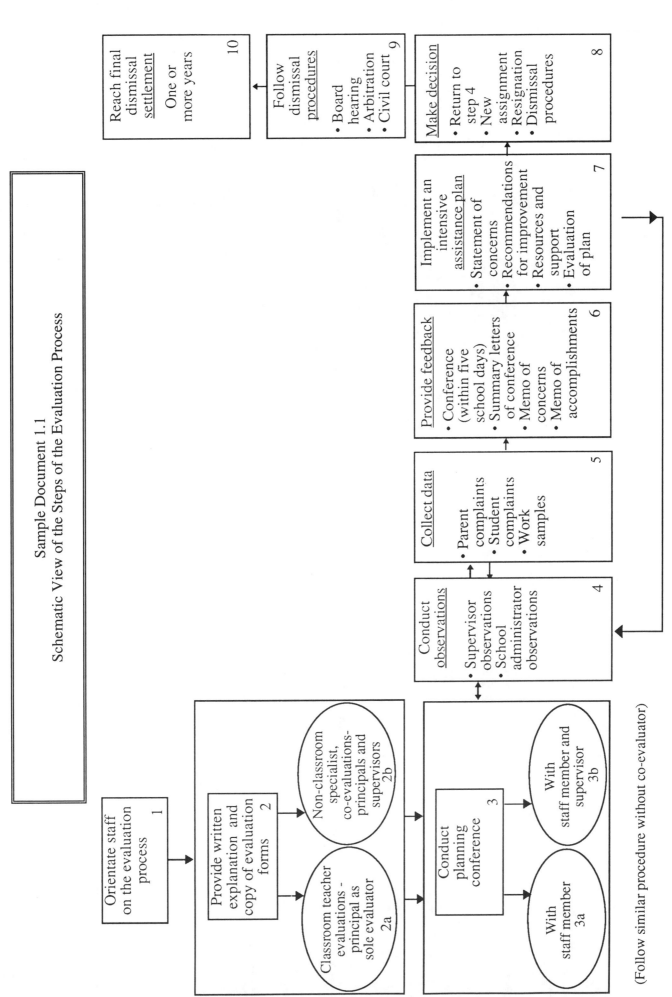

1 Orientate staff on the evaluation process

2 Provide written explanation and copy of evaluation forms

2a Classroom teacher evaluations - principal as sole evaluator

2b Non-classroom specialist, co-evaluations- principals and supervisors

3 Conduct planning conference

3a With staff member

3b With staff member and supervisor

4 Conduct observations
• Supervisor observations
• School administrator observations

5 Collect data
• Parent complaints
• Student complaints
• Work samples

6 Provide feedback
• Conference (within five school days)
• Summary letters of conference
• Memo of concerns
• Memo of accomplishments

7 Implement an intensive assistance plan
• Statement of concerns
• Recommendations for improvement
• Resources and support
• Evaluation of plan

8 Make decision
• Return to step 4
• New assignment
• Resignation
• Dismissal procedures

9 Follow dismissal procedures
• Board hearing
• Arbitration
• Civil court

10 Reach final dismissal settlement
One or more years

Stages 4 through 7 may be repeated throughout the process.

(Follow similar procedure without co-evaluator)

2 Establishing the Foundation for the Evaluation Process

The school district must develop and implement consistent evaluation procedures for all staff members.

Suggested Timeline: August

The school district must take the necessary steps to establish the foundation for consistent evaluation procedures for all employees prior to the start of the staff evaluation process. The first major step is the development of job descriptions for all district employees that are maintained by the district personnel office. Even though formats may vary, job descriptions summarize the most important features of the job, including a description of the work, worker characteristics, responsibilities, and reporting structure (Society for Human Resource Management, 1994, p. 43). A job description for a guidance counselor is shown in Sample Document 2.1. Samples of job descriptions for other specialist positions are available through various organizations including the National School Boards Association. Descriptions must be periodically updated to reflect any changes in duties and responsibilities, and these changes must be sent to school administrators and supervisors for their reference. Because staff members in your school may be unaware of the duties and responsibilities of the specialists, the staff handbook should include a section with the job descriptions of all employees. Also, a procedure to verify that each staff member has received a copy of the job description that applies to his or her own position must be developed. One way would be to number the staff handbooks and have each staff member sign a form stating that he or she has received the document. This documentation should be maintained in the school personnel file. In addition, the chief personnel director of the school district must effectuate plans for school administrators to consistently supervise and evaluate all staff members. When you evaluate or coevaluate a specialist, you must inform him or her of the name and title of the other evaluator. Even though some specialists may be assigned to several schools, and thus may be evaluated by more than one school administrator or supervisor, consistent procedures must be established and followed. Also, you and the coevaluator(s) must be able to show that all specialists are treated consistently throughout schools in the district. If some specialists are treated differently than other specialists, they may have cause for legal challenge in civil court because your actions may be considered arbitrary, capricious, and unreasonable. Although there is no 100% guarantee of winning an unsatisfactory evaluation of a specialist, you must meet the just-cause requirements. A third-party hearing officer, an arbitrator, or the civil court is unlikely to overturn your case if you can answer "yes" to the following questions that are asked to determine if the just-cause requirements have been met:

1. Did you and the coevaluator make known the evaluation process for the school district to all school specialists working at the school(s)?
   Yes_____ No_____

2. Did you and the coevaluator apply the evaluation procedures consistently to all school specialists throughout the school district?
   Yes_____ No_____

3. Did you and the coevaluator treat all staff members consistently and not single out the school specialist?
   Yes_____ No_____

4. Did you and the coevaluator observe all phases of the school specialist's assignments?
   Yes_____ No_____

5. Did you or the coevaluator keep a continuous and accurately dated file of all conferences and observations?
   Yes_____ No_____

6. Did you and the coevaluator give the school specialist written memoranda of concerns specifying the exact deficiencies?
   Yes_____ No_____

7. In each memorandum of concerns given to the school specialist, did you or the coevaluator state or list specific suggestions for correcting deficiencies and how to achieve a satisfactory level of performance?
   Yes_____ No_____

8. Did you and the coevaluator give the school specialist a reasonable period of time to improve performance?
   Yes_____ No_____

9. Did you and the coevaluator establish an intensive assistance plan for the school specialist that uses school and district resources?
   Yes_____ No_____

10. Did you and the coevaluator inform the school specialist that failure to achieve an acceptable level of performance by a specified date would result in an issuance of an unsatisfactory evaluation?
    Yes_____ No_____

Unless you answer "yes" to these 10 questions, you may not have met the just-cause requirements and you may lose your unsatisfactory evaluation case. As a result, the specialist is likely to remain on your staff and may revel in your failure to dismiss him or her.

The need to meet just cause does not exist unless you anticipate recommending the nonrenewal or dismissal of a staff member. Nevertheless, there are some steps that you must take to lay the foundation should it become necessary to make such a recommendation. Therefore, before the school year begins, the personnel department must provide all principals with a list of the specialists who will be working in their schools and the name of the supervisor for each specialist. This should also include the names of other school assignments for specialists that work at more than one site. In addition, the list should include the specialist's hire date and tenure date, if applicable.

At the school level, plans for evaluation should be well underway. There should be a basic plan that includes a tentative schedule and procedures for communicating with other staff involved in evaluating specialists (e.g., assistant principals, supervisors), welcoming staff back to school, and providing orientation to set a positive tone with expectations and a commitment to work together for the benefit of the students (Lawrence, Vachon, Leake, & Leake, 1993, p. 8). At the beginning of the school year, you may not know which, if any, specialist is performing below an acceptable level of performance; however, when you and the coevaluator recognize the need to focus on a particular specialist, you will further refine the tentative schedule and use the calendar format shown in Resource A.

During the month of August, you, as well as other school administrators in your district, should make sure that the following occur consistently:

❑ Review the information provided by the district's personnel department listing staff members assigned to your school and note their tenure designation. (Tenured employees have just-cause rights that require more stringent documentation should a recommendation for nonrenewal or dismissal be made based on job performance.)

❑ Review the most recent job descriptions for specialist positions to ensure that the observation/evaluation forms you plan to use are consistent and up-to-date.

❑ Include job description information in the staff handbook along with general staff evaluation information (see Sample Document 2.1).

❑ About 3 weeks before school starts, send a welcome letter to all staff assigned to the building (see Sample Document 2.2).

❑ Assign a "buddy" staff member to each new staff member, and identify the "buddy" staff member in a welcome letter to the new staff member (see Sample Document 2.3).

❑ Provide orientation for "buddy" staff members assigned to assist new staff members. The orientation should include the following:

   1. Review of specific building rules and procedures;

   2. Suggested timeline for interacting with the new staff member;

   3. Discussion of "what ifs" (e.g., what if the new staff member is experiencing problems with his or her assignment or what if the new staff member and "buddy" staff member are incompatible); and

   4. Suggestions regarding the type of assistance the "buddy" staff member can provide to the new staff member.

❑ Provide an orientation session for the entire staff (including guidance counselors, social workers, psychologists, teaching assistants, secretary, engineer). These sessions should highlight the educational philosophy of the school, district goals, and expectations for staff. If possible, this session should also include opportunities for the staff members to socialize with each other.

❑ Review contractual language, school board rules, state statutes, and the U.S. Constitution (e.g., Fourteenth Amendment) to ensure that due process is followed and that the property rights of staff members are not violated.

❑ Develop a tentative calendar outlining the key actions to be completed by the specialist's evaluators (see Resource A).

❑ Meet with your assistant principal(s) to discuss the evaluation process.

❑ Meet with the supervisors for specialists to discuss the evaluation process, particularly if the job performance of a specialist is unsatisfactory.

❑ Establish a consistent plan to evaluate all personnel who work in the school.

Administrative Tips to Remember

❑ When pairing a "buddy" staff member and a new staff member, consider the value of matching individuals as closely as possible based on similarities in gender, personality, and experience.

❑ Periodically, review questions on just-cause requirements that you may be asked during the unsatisfactory evaluation process.

❑ If you are the coevaluator of specialists with another principal or supervisor, make sure consistent evaluation procedures are followed.

❑ Do not use hearsay evidence to document an unsatisfactory evaluation.

❑ Expect that the completion of the dismissal process will take more than one year.

JOB DESCRIPTION

TITLE: Guidance Counselor - Elementary School Focus

REPORTS TO: Principal and/or Supervisor

OBJECTIVE   To provide guidance and counseling services in a variety of settings in
OF POSITION: an effort to help students and their families overcome problems that interfere
                with learning and to assist students as they strive to become mature,
                educated, productive, and responsible citizens.

DUTIES AND RESPONSIBILITIES:

1. Provide group and individual counseling to students in an effort to enhance the personal growth, self-understanding, and maturity of students.

2. Work with students on an individual basis in an effort to solve personal problems relative to the home environment, family relations, health, and emotional adjustment.

3. Communicate with parents as needed in writing and through telephone conferences, as well as in face-to-face conference.

4. Maintain accurate records of counseling sessions with students and any meetings with their parents/guardians.

5. Provide assistance to students to help them discover and develop their special abilities and talents.

6. Assist in the orientation of new staff members relative to guidance issues and procedures.

7. Provide in-service training in guidance for teachers and student teachers in assigned school(s) including, but not limited to, the services offered through the division of student services, such as standardized assessment, maintenance of student records, and report preparation.

8. Enroll students new to the school and provide orientation for them relative to school policies, procedures, and the educational program.

9. Oversee the local school application process in relation to the district-wide school selection process.

10. Coordinate the application process (including recommendations from other staff members) for students participating in special opportunity programs.

11. Coordinate the after-school and weekend tutor program.

12. Coordinate the referral process for students believed to have exceptional education needs as well as students believed to have non-exceptional education needs.

13. Coordinate the standardized testing program, which includes receiving testing materials, ensuring procedures are followed, maintaining confidentiality of materials, and returning materials to the district office.

14. Provide assistance to faculty members relative to the interpretation of individual standardized test scores, composite test scores, and other pertinent data.

15. Coordinate the local School to Work Program, which includes: a) maintaining up-to-date occupational information for distribution to individual students as well as to classes studying occupations, and (b) coordinating field trips into the community.

16. Advise administrators and faculty on matters of student discipline.

17. Remain proactive by conferring regularly with staff members relative to potential problems students may be having.

18. Provide guidance to students relative to their participation in school and community activities.

19. Play a key role in interpreting the objectives of the school's educational program to students and their parents/guardians.

20. Interpret the guidance program to the community as a whole.

21. Maintain and protect the confidentiality of student records and cumulative folders.

22. Complete other related duties as assigned.

Date

Dear Staff:

I hope you are having a restful and pleasant summer vacation. The 00XX-00XX school year will present new challenges to all of us—new students, new staff members, new courses, and new technology such as Internet accessibility, which will be incorporated into classroom instruction.

This school year will provide an opportunity for us to develop innovative techniques and strategies as well as to implement creative ideas to serve all of our children. As always, we must continue to work together to make _____ the best school in the _____ School District.

With much enthusiasm, I look forward to working with you this school year and meeting the challenges that lie ahead as we prepare our students to be productive citizens far into the 21st century.

Again, welcome back! This will be the best year ever at _____ School. I look forward to seeing you soon.

Sincerely,

_____
Principal

Sample Document 2.3
Letter Assigning a "Buddy" Staff Member to Each New and Transfer Staff Member
(Place on school letterhead)

Date

Name of Specialist
and Address

Dear _____:

I want to extend a warm and special welcome to _____ School. I want to make this an educationally rewarding and successful school year for you. This will be the best year for students, parents, and staff at _____ School.

As you know, the beginning of the school year is a busy time for all of us. To help you adjust to your new school, I have assigned _____ to serve as your "buddy" staff member and to answer questions you may have. I am also here to assist you in any way possible to make this a successful school year. Please feel free to contact me to discuss any concerns you may have as you begin your new assignment.

Again, welcome to _____ School. I am happy that you have joined our staff, and I look forward to working with you this year.

Sincerely,

_____
Principal

3 Beginning the Evaluation Process

If clarification is needed, don't be afraid to seek district and legal counsel to interpret the evaluation sections of the master contract.

Suggested Timeline: September

As the school administrator, you should orient your staff to the purpose and methods of the evaluation process. There are common expectations, particularly as related to due process, that cut across all evaluation procedures. Therefore, within the school district and at any individual school, all staff members should receive the same consideration. For example, you must provide a written description of the observation forms and the projected timeline to complete the evaluation process (Lawrence, Vachon, Leake, & Leake, p. 13). Still, there are some differences in the contractual provisions of the master contract that governs the evaluation of various groups of staff members, including special education teachers and specialists assigned to nonclassroom duties and responsibilities. Because a specialist may work in nonclassroom settings with students who have special needs, consider coevaluating the specialist with his or her supervisor. Often, the supervisor has knowledge and expertise that will complement your background and experience as you evaluate the specialist's job performance. When you are conducting an evaluation that may lead to nonrenewal or dismissal, the coevaluation arrangement is particularly important.

At the beginning of the school year, you, as the school administrator, must send a letter to the specialist identifying yourself and the specialist's supervisor as the coevaluators. And, if you have an assistant principal in your building, include him or her as an evaluator. The assistant principal will be useful in supplementing the process by making informal observations and providing assistance as necessary. You must follow a consistent plan to evaluate the specialist.

If you believe that the specialist has a performance deficiency, you and the coevaluator must agree on the problems that exist. In that way, you are more likely to help the specialist to improve his or her performance.

If you are the principal, you will probably spend more time observing the specialist than the specialist's supervisor because you are located in the school on a daily basis. If you are the specialist's supervisor, you may have a different perspective on the job that the specialist is performing. You both must be aware of differences in perceptions and possibly conflicting agendas. Any differences must be resolved early in the process to ensure that you are both working together and are not sending mixed messages to the specialist. For example, you should plan to jointly conduct some conferences with the specialist and make sure that you are sending the same message. Even though your individual styles may differ, you both should discuss and agree to general procedures, such as the format of meetings and conferences with the specialist.

For the pre-observation conference, you may agree that you will

- Maintain a businesslike atmosphere
- Use the preobservation conference form to focus the discussion and to find out as much about the context of what you will observe
- Use questions to encourage the specialist to talk and elaborate rather than to respond with a "yes" or "no"
- Close the conference by restating the date, time, and any other specifics about the logistics of your observation

When planning and conducting the post-observation conference, you may agree that you will

- Emphasize performance, not personal qualities
- Use firsthand observations or information
- Describe actual behaviors, not attributes
- Be specific and concrete
- Be objective and keep an open mind
- Clearly describe the consequences of unacceptable job performance
- Provide a manageable amount of information
- Summarize and document the discussion in a letter
- Include provisions for follow-up
- Recommend specific responses to any directives not for specialist's discretion
- Obtain a commitment from the specialist for some concrete change in job performance, not just a willingness to "think about it"

- Near the end of the conference, summarize any points the specialist should remember
- Emphasize the specialist's responsibility for improved performance

During the postobservation conference, you may agree to

- Maintain a businesslike atmosphere
- Use the observation form to focus the discussion and to inform the specialist about what you observed (if the specialist has also completed an observation form, compare your perceptions)
- Use questions that will encourage the specialist to talk and elaborate, rather than questions require only a "yes" or "no" response
- Close the conference by restating expectations and resources and support that is available

After the conference you should also agree on who should follow up on certain actions. If you and the coevaluator make recommendations, you must decide who will check to see if the specialist implemented them. Likewise, if you both promised to provide support (e.g., resource materials, visitation to another school), you must decide who will follow through with the necessary arrangements.

The poor performance of an incompetent specialist is marked by key characteristics that occur excessively because of one or more of the following factors: inadequate training; personal problems that interfere with effective job performance; negative attitude, refusal to do what is expected, or both. The profile of an incompetent specialist may include any combination of the following characteristics:

- Consumes too much administrative time
- Displays a negative attitude toward students
- Does not adequately supervise students
- Does not follow school procedures and guidelines
- Does not adhere to federal, state, or district policies or all three
- Does not prepare or plan adequately
- Does not use time efficiently
- Has problems relating to students
- Does not communicate effectively with parents
- Engages in power struggles with administration
- Has a limited range of strategies for dealing with situations
- Has numerous complaints from students, parents, and colleagues
- Has poor management skills
- Is resistant to change
- Is uncooperative with other staff members
- Lacks communication skills

- Lacks organizational skills
- Has excessive manifestations of poor judgment

During September, you should complete the following:

❏ Provide a written explanation of the evaluation process, and include a sample of the observation and evaluation forms that you and the co-evaluator will use (see Sample Documents 3.1, 3.2, 3.3, and 3.4). (Note: Because a job description for a guidance counselor was used in Sample Document 2.1, the observation forms referenced here are also designed for a guidance counselor. The job description, district expectations, and observation forms should agree.)

❏ Begin conducting informal evaluations during the first week of the school year, so that you can identify potential areas of concern and maintain a daily summary of observations (see Sample Documents 3.2 and 3.5).

❏ Hand deliver the evaluator identification letter to each staff member, identifying yourself as the evaluator and supplying a roster for the staff member to sign or initial to show receipt of the letter. If a supervisor is coevaluating the staff member/specialist include the name of both evaluators in the letter. Check the master contract for your school district to see if both evaluators must sign the letter (see Sample Documents 3.6 and 3.7).

❏ Establish a routine for informing the specialist about your evaluation comments.

❏ Prepare a parental complaint file for both verbal and written complaints for each specialist (see Sample Document 3.8).

❏ Keep copies of all notes that specialists write you.

❏ Plan to provide written feedback on performance to specialists and teachers within 5 school days.

❏ Provide professional tips in the weekly staff bulletin.

❏ Hold meetings for all staff members, including specialists, and for the supervisor for each specialist as appropriate.

❏ Provide ongoing assistance and support to all staff members.

❏ Set up a filing system to accumulate various forms of documentation that reflect the performance of each staff member.

❏ Use the evaluation forms that were negotiated with the specialist's association, if applicable.

❏ Conduct a reasonable number of observations and hold feedback conferences followed by written response each month.

❏ Always allow staff members an opportunity to appeal the observation/evaluation by including a written attachment to the observation/evaluation form.

❏ Inform the specialist of his or her right to have representation at meetings related to performance evaluation.

Administrative Tips to Remember

- ❑ Do not place the letter identifying the evaluator in the staff member's mail box. You may need proof that the specialist received the evaluation letter.

- ❑ Work in collaboration with the specialist's supervisor, your assistant principal, and any other district administration staff who can conduct performance evaluations.

- ❑ Remember that you, as principal, can coevaluate specialists or special education teachers working at more than one site.

- ❑ To handle serious parental complaints, use the misconduct provision of the contract, if one exists.

- ❑ Make sure that the evaluation procedures for specialists and special education teachers are consistent with those of general education teachers.

- ❑ Do not allow a member in the same bargaining unit to be involved in the evaluation of a peer unless it is specified in the master contract.

- ❑ Do not base your evaluation on hearsay, but use firsthand observations, evaluation information or both.

- ❑ Complete all sections of the observation/evaluation form before you sign it.

Sample Document 3.1
Memorandum Explaining the Evaluation Process for Staff Members Serving in Specialist Positions
(Place on school letterhead)

Date:

To: Specialist

From: Principal

Re: Evaluation of Staff Members Serving in Specialist Positions

This memorandum explains procedures that will be used when conducting evaluations of staff members who serve in specialist positions. The overall purpose of staff evaluation is to improve job performance and to promote professional growth of staff members. To achieve these goals, part of the evaluation process will involve identifying strengths and weaknesses in performance, and then providing suggestions for improving weak areas. Specialists will be coevaluated by their principal and their supervisor. If a specialist works at one school, the principal and his/her supervisor will conduct the evaluation. If the specialist works in more than one school, the principals at both schools and the specialist's supervisors will conduct the evaluation. The following procedures will be used to evaluate specialists this year:

Step 1--Pre-Observation Communication (Formative)

Formal observations will be conducted for specialists scheduled for a mandatory evaluation. Formal evaluation may also be conducted for specialists not scheduled for an evaluation. At the beginning of the school year, the principal, specialist's supervisor, and specialist will meet to discuss job duties and responsibilities as well as to talk about job expectations for the school year. At this pre-observation conference, the specialist will be provided with further clarification of the evaluation process and procedures, a copy of his or her job description, and any variation in forms that will be used at the work site. Forms that will be used include the Pre-Observation Planning Form, Informal Observation Form, and Formal Observation/Conference Summary Form.

Step 2--Self-Evaluation Component (Formative)

Because self-evaluation is a major component of the evaluation process for staff members, each specialist will conduct a self-analysis using a copy of the appropriate evaluation form. Prior to the post-observation conference, the specialist is to check the category that best describes his or her performance. The specialist's self-evaluation is designed to assist the staff member in reflecting on his or her performance. The self-evaluation form will not be placed in his or her district personnel file.

Step 3--Observation and Post-Observation Conference (Formative)

The specialist and the coevaluators will complete Part A of the evaluation form. During the first month of the school year, a post-observation conference will be held with the specialist to discuss his or her performance and compare the self-evaluation form with the evaluation forms completed by the coevaluators. Strengths, limitations, and suggestions for improvement, if necessary, will also be discussed. Based on the number of suggestions for improvement, the coevaluators and specialist will determine a schedule for discussing progress being made in identified areas.

Step 4--Year-End Evaluation (Summative)

This is the final evaluation conference of the school year, and it will be held during April or May. After the conference, comments will be placed on the district evaluation form. The specialist will be asked to read the evaluation, check a box to indicate agreement or disagreement, and sign the form. If the specialist disagrees with the evaluation, he or she may attach a written response to the evaluation form and return the form along with any comments to the principal within three school days. The specialist's signature does not necessarily mean that he or she agrees with the evaluation, but that the evaluation process has been completed. Then, a copy of the completed evaluation form will be sent to the personnel department and placed in the specialist's file.

If you have any questions, please contact my secretary to make an appointment to see me.

cc: Specialist's Supervisor

INFORMAL OBSERVATION FORM
(Observation time: less than 15 minutes)

Date_____ Start of Observation_____ End of Observation_____

Specialist's Name_____ Title_____

School Assignment _____ Non-Tenured _____ Tenured _____

Rating Scale
E=Excellent, S=Satisfactory, M=Marginal, U=Unsatisfactory, N/A=Not Applicable

Part A. Working Relationship With Others

	E	S	M	U	N/A
1. With students					
2. With parents					
3. With teachers					
4. With staff					
5. With administrators					
6. With supervisors					

Part B. Professional Responsibilities of a _____

	E	S	M	U	N/A
(Note to Evaluators: The criteria listed in this section should be consistent with the job description and district expectations:					
1.					
2.					
3.					
4.					
5.					
6.					

Part C. Strengths, Limitations, and Recommendations

    1. Specialist's Strengths:

    2. Specialist's Limitations:

    3. Recommendations for Improvement:

Observer's Signature and Title_____

Sample Document 3.3
Pre-Observation Conference Planning Form
(Place on school letterhead)

PRE-OBSERVATION WORKSHEET
(To be completed by the specialist for discussion with the observer prior to a scheduled observation.)

Specialist's Name _____ Title _____

Observer's Name _____ Title _____

Activity to be Observed_____

Date of Observation _____ Time _____

List the specific objectives for the activity that will be observed.
1.

2.

3.

4.

List the strategies that will be used to accomplish the objectives.

List how you will measure if the objectives are met.

List any circumstances or problems about which the observer should know.

List any special things you want the observer to monitor.

Plans for lesson/activity available for review. ☐ Yes ☐ No
Comments

Other comments.

Specialist's Signature _____ Date _____

Observer's Signature _____ Date _____
(Signature only implies that information has been discussed.)

FORMAL OBSERVATION/CONFERENCE SUMMARY FORM
(Observation time: 15 minutes or more)

Part A. Basic Information

Conference Date _____ Start of Conference _____ End of Conference _____

Specialist's Name _____ Title _____

School Assignment _____ Non-Tenured _____ Tenured _____

Observation Date(s) and Times _____ _____

_____ _____

Responsibilities and Duties Observed:

_____

_____

_____

_____

Rating Scale for Parts B and C

E=Excellent, S=Satisfactory, M=Marginal, U=Unsatisfactory, N/A=Not Applicable

Part B. Working Relationship With Others	Rating Scale				
	E	S	M	U	N/A
1. With students					
2. With parents					
3. With teachers					
4. With staff					
5. With administrators					
6. With supervisors					

Part C. Professional Responsibilities of a _____	Rating Scale				
	E	S	M	U	N/A
(Note to Evaluators: The criteria listed in this section should be consistent with the job description and district expectations)					
1.					
2.					
3.					
4.					
5.					
6.					
7.					
8.					
9.					
10.					
11.					
12					
13.					
14.					
15.					
16.					
17.					
18.					
19.					
20.					
21.					
22.					
23.					

Part C. Professional Responsibilities of a _____	Rating Scale				
CONTINUED	E	S	M	U	N/A
24.					
25.					
26.					
27.					
28.					
29.					
30.					

Part D. Strengths, Limitations, and Recommendations

1. Specialist's Strengths:

2. Specialist's Limitations:

3. Recommendations for Improvement:

Part E. Overall Assessment

   1. Evaluator(s) Comments

   2. Evaluator(s) Rating

     ☐ Excellent   ☐ Satisfactory   ☐ Marginal   ☐ Unsatisfactory

Part F. Joint Signatures

Note to Specialist: Your signature indicates that the conference has been held and that you have seen this report. If you disagree with this assessment of your job performance, you may attach a written response to this form. Return this form -- along with any response -- within three school days, and I will forward it the personnel department, where it will be placed in your file.

Specialist's Signature_____ Date_____

Supervisor's Signature_____ Date_____

Principal's Signature_____ Date_____

SUMMARY OF OBSERVATIONS OF STAFF MEMBERS
_____ 00XX

SCHOOL_____   PRINCIPAL_____

(Insert the dates that school is in session along the top row, and write the names of all staff members in the first column. Place the initials of the administrator or supervisor in the grid to indicate that an observation was made and by whom. Circle the initials for a formal observation or use a check mark for an informal observation.)

STAFF MEMBER																															

Sample Document 3.6
Letter Identifying the Specialist's Evaluator(s)
(Place on school letterhead)

Date

Name of Specialist and
School Address

Dear_____:

The primary purpose of evaluation is to improve job performance and to promote professional development. Evaluation is a cooperative process for improving and maintaining the quality of the educational program in the school district. Staff members should view the evaluation as a learning experience and as a way for both the staff member and the administrator to grow in understanding and knowledge. This is consistent with the contract between the _____ Board of Education and the (name of the association). The evaluation procedures for this school year will ensure that a cooperative plan is established by the staff member and his or her evaluator(s).

Section ____ (Paragraph _) of the _____ contract states that the identification of the evaluator(s) must be made known to the staff member by name and title by the third Friday in September of the school year. Accordingly, you are informed that your performance during the 00XX-00XX school year will be co-evaluated by _____, _____ supervisor, and me, with possible collaboration with other administrative and supervisory staff assigned to _____ School. In the event that someone else must serve in my capacity or in _____'s capacity, the evaluation will be conducted by that person.

If you have any questions about the evaluation process, please contact me.

Sincerely,

_____
Principal

cc: Specialist's Supervisor

```
┌─────────────────────────────────────────────────────────────────────┐
│                      Sample Document 3.7                             │
│  Roster for Staff Members' Signatures Acknowledging Receipt of       │
│                Letter Identifying Evaluator(s)                        │
│                  (Place on school letterhead)                        │
└─────────────────────────────────────────────────────────────────────┘
```

_____ SCHOOL

_____, _____, 00XX

STAFF ROSTER

SIGNATURE	NAME
_____	_____
_____	_____
_____	_____
_____	_____
_____	_____
_____	_____
_____	_____
_____	_____
_____	_____
_____	_____
_____	_____
_____	_____
_____	_____
_____	_____
_____	_____
_____	_____
_____	_____

*NOTE TO STAFF: Your signature verifies that you received a copy of your Evaluator
                  Identification Letter.

```
┌─────────────────────────────────────────────────┐
│                                                 │
│              Sample Document 3.8                │
│               Parental Complaints               │
│                                                 │
└─────────────────────────────────────────────────┘
```

You must have a procedure for recording parental complaints and maintaining a file for related documents that can be used to support an unsatisfactory evaluation. If there are contractual procedures for handling parental complaints, you must follow those procedures. Such procedures may include informing the staff member of the nature of the parental complaint, investigating the complaint, resolving the complaint, and giving a copy of the disposition to the staff member.

Procedures:

- ☐ Use a standard parental complaint form for parents to register complaint.
- ☐ Investigate the complaint as appropriate.
- ☐ Resolve the complaint.
- ☐ Follow contractual procedures for informing the staff member with regard to the disposition of the matter.
- ☐ Maintain a parental complaint file with a copy of the complaint, your disposition, and the staff member's response.

Administrative Tips to Remember

- ☐ If a parent submits a letter of complaint instead of completing the parental complaint form, attach a copy of the form to the letter and fill in any information, as needed.
- ☐ For serious parental complaints, use the misconduct provision of the contract if one exists.

_____ SCHOOL
PARENTAL COMPLAINT FORM

Date_____Time_____a.m./p.m.

Student_____Grade_____ID Number_____

Address_____

Person Filing Complaint_____

Relationship to Student_____

Phone Number - Home_____ Other_____

Nature of Complaint_____

_____

_____

_____

Action Requested_____

_____

Has a Previous Complaint Been Filed? Yes_____   No_____   Date_____

Person(s) Spoken to:

_____
                          Name/Title/Department

_____
                          Name/Title/Department
Resolution_____

_____

_____

_____

_____

Complaint Resolved___   Further Action Necessary_____

_____   _____
           Signature/Title   Date

Date

Name of Specialist and
School Address

Dear_____:

Section ____ (Paragraph __) of the _____ School District Contract states that when a parental or public complaint is filed against a staff member, the individual staff member must be notified of the complaint. Consequently, I am forwarding the attached parental complaint/letter that I received about you on _____, 00XX.

My secretary will schedule a meeting for you to meet with me to discuss this parental complaint by _____, 00XX.

Sincerely,

_____

Principal

4 *Identifying the School Specialist in Need of Intensive Assistance*

Don't assume that specialists perceive things the same way that you do.

Suggested Timeline: October

As the principal or supervisor, you must identify staff members who need assistance, including specialists who work in nonclassroom assignments. Moreover, you must evaluate specialists regardless of the setting in which they work: large groups, small groups, one-to-one, in public meetings, or in confidential sessions. You must resist any reluctance to evaluate specialists because they use unfamiliar educational jargon, have degrees in fields in which you may have little or no knowledge, or have impressive sounding job titles. As the principal, you are qualified to identify incompetent specialists—regardless of your own certification. Clearly, you can recognize the difference between acceptable or unacceptable levels of job performance regardless of the specialist's position. Nevertheless, because of cases in which you might recommend dismissal due to incompetence, you should coevaluate the specialist with a supervisor in the specialist's area. This will help ensure that appropriate assistance was provided and will counter accusations that you have little or no expertise in the specialist's area.

At this point, you may still need to think about the characteristics of the coevaluators because of accusations that might be made as a strategy by the specialist's representative during an unsatisfactory evaluation case. For example, you must be sensitive to the gender and racial make-up of the coevaluators, such as two white males coevaluating an African American female specialist or two white males coevaluating a Hispanic female specialist. This is especially true if the evaluation may lead to dismissal. In fact, you will want to prevent situations that will provide the specialist's representative with the opportunity to cloud the issue with race or gender rather than focusing on the specialist's poor performance. Also, be aware that other discrimination issues may center on age, religion, and violations of First and Fourteenth Amendment rights.

Nevertheless, some specialists receive tenure because they performed at acceptable levels for many years. In fact, their personnel files probably contain evaluation reports from principals and supervisors that clearly indicate that the specialist was competent when recommended to continue as an employee of the school district. Furthermore, many of these specialists may have even received excellent evaluations. But personal problems may be interfering with a specialist's performance (e.g., drugs, alcohol, poor health, death in the family, mental disease, financial hardship), or the specialist may feel the need to change professions. As coevaluators, you and the specialist's supervisor must be sensitive to special situations and be completely fair with the specialist whose external problems may be factors causing unsatisfactory job performance. Still, you must base your evaluation decision on placing the educational needs of children first.

You must also be aware of the fact that, in addition to direct observation of the specialist's performance, other indicators of ineffective performance include information from various sources. These sources include statistics that reflect the number of student discipline referrals and the number of students not responding to services, as well as the number of complaints from students, parents, and other staff members. The specialist's attitude, lack of support for school initiatives, resistance to change, and uncooperativeness with other staff members also are indicators. As you know, the documentation necessary to dismiss the nontenured specialist is less stringent than that required to dismiss a specialist who has tenure. Moreover, the procedure to dismiss a tenured specialist requires an extensive amount of time and documentation.

During September and October, the following should occur:

❑ Continue to observe activities that are occurring throughout the school so you can identify specialists who may be experiencing problems.

❑ Prior to formal observations of a specialist who is receiving intensive assistance, hold a preobservation conference with the specialist to discuss his or her plans and the expected outcomes for the activity or event you will observe (see Sample Document 3.3).

❑ Provide feedback that includes limitations and recommendations for improvement; then give a reasonable amount of time for the specialist to accomplish these improvements.

❑ Write a memorandum of concerns that includes suggestions for improvements. Then hold a postobservation conference to discuss the concerns (see Sample Document 4.1).

❑ Provide an opportunity for the specialist to observe a specialist in the same school (see Sample Document 4.2).

❑ Provide an opportunity for the specialist to shadow a successful specialist at another school for an entire day (see Sample Document 4.3).

❑ Provide an opportunity for the specialist from another school to work with the specialist in your school (see Sample Document 4.4).

❑ Provide articles for the specialist to read (see Sample Document 4.5).

❑ Refer the specialist to appropriate sections in the staff handbook (see Sample Document 4.6).

❑ Provide opportunities for the specialist to attend workshops conducted by the school district (see Sample Document 4.7).

❑ Examine the convention booklet for the specialist's association to identify sessions to recommend for the specialist to attend (see Sample Document 4.8).

❑ Continue maintaining a parental complaint file (both verbal and written) for each specialist (see Sample Document 3.8).

❑ If the specialist does not improve, write a letter to the specialist summarizing the postobservation conference (see Sample Document 4.9).

❑ If the specialist is showing improvement, note that on the observation form, but re-emphasize the suggestions for improvement that you previously gave to the specialist.

❑ Within a reasonable time, inform the specialist of your assessment of your observation (for example, 5 school days.)

❑ Continue keeping copies of all notes that you write to the specialist about his or her problems or other school-related issues.

❑ Issue a letter to the specialist reviewing assistance provided to him or her (see Sample Document 4.10).

❑ Send a memorandum to the district office requesting observation of and assistance for the specialist (see Sample Document 4.11).

❑ Send a memorandum to your supervisor summarizing observations, conferences, and support provided to the specialist (see Sample Document 4.12).

❑ Write a memorandum of accomplishment to determine if the specialist achieved the recommendations (see Sample Document 4.13).

❑ Begin to prepare an unsatisfactory evaluation binder. This should have a cover page, table of contents, and a divider for each section (see Sample Documents 4.14 and 4.15).

❑ Check pertinent historical information about the specialist's background in the district (see Sample Document 4.16).

Administrative Tips to Remember

❏ If possible, check to see if the specialist enrolled in the suggested workshops/classes.

❏ Ensure that resources are available to the specialist to make improvements.

❏ Give the specialist a reasonable amount of time to improve (e.g., 30 days).

❏ Inform the specialist in writing about the right to have representation at meetings.

You and the coevaluator must conduct weekly informal and formal observations/evaluations to assess the performance of the specialist and communicate your findings to him or her. If there are performance problems, write a memorandum of concerns to the specialist about his or her performance. You must accurately record the dates and times of your observations and what you observed. Also, you must clearly list your concerns about the specialist's performance and include at least one example under each area of concern. Listed below are examples of phrases that you can use to describe performance problems:

• has not maintained	• was not consistent
• was not always prepared	• inaccurately diagnosed
• did not monitor	• failed to implement
• failed to improve	• had not been
• failed to follow	• failed to have
• provided insufficient	• proceeded without proper
• consistently failed to	• did not have
• has made no substantial improvement	• caused friction between
• did not exhibit	• failed to communicate
• caused dissension	• neglected to
• failed to be	• exhibited an inability to
• failed to produce	• refused to follow
• disregarded	• displayed negative

Sample Document 4.1 (continued)
Memorandum of Concerns and Recommendations
(Place on school letterhead)

(This letter can be easily adapted when it is sent by both coevaluators.)

Date:

To: Specialist's Name

From: Principal's Name

Re: Concerns and Recommendations for Improvement

This memorandum of concerns is to inform you about my concerns relative to your performance as a _____ at _____ School and to provide recommendations to help you improve. They are as follows:

Concern # 1 *(State concern and give an example.)*

    Recommendations *(Be specific and concise.)*

    A.

    B.

    C.

    D.

Comments

Concern # 2 *(State concern and give an example.)*

Recommendations *(Be specific and concise.)*

A.

B.

C.

D.

Comments

Concern # 3 *(State concern and give an example.)*

Recommendations *(Be specific and concise.)*

A.

B.

C.

D.

Comments

Recommendations *(Be specific and concise.)*

A.

B.

C.

D.

Comments

I stand ready to support the improvement of your performance as a specialist, but the responsibility for that improvement clearly rests with you. If you have any questions about this memorandum or if you disagree with my concerns and recommendations, you must inform me in writing no later than _____, __, 00XX, or you may see my secretary to schedule a meeting with me to discuss this memorandum.

Sample Document 4.2
Letter Confirming Arrangements for the Specialist to Observe a Specialist at the Same School
(Place on school letterhead)

(This letter can be easily adapted when it is sent by both coevaluators.)

Date

Name of Specialist and
Name of School

Dear _____:

I want you to have the opportunity to improve your job performance as the _____
at _____ School. As your evaluator, I am concerned about how you deal
with students and teachers. I would like you to shadow _____,
_____ to observe how he/she works as a guidance counselor with his/her students and
teachers.

    (List specific activities, e.g., planning, general organization.)

Again, I am ready to assist in making this school year a successful experience for you.

Sincerely,

_____

Principal

cc: Specialist's Supervisor

Sample Document 4.3
Letter Confirming Arrangements for the Specialist to Shadow a Specialist in Another School
(Place on school letterhead)

(This letter can be easily adapted when it is sent by both coevaluators.)

Date

Name of Specialist and
Name of School

Dear _____:

I want you to have a successful experience as the _____ at
_____ School. As we have discussed earlier, opportunities are available for
you to observe at other schools in the _____ School District. Thus,
I have made arrangements for you to spend an entire day at _____
School, which is located at _____.

You are to report to _____ School on _____, 00XX. You will
spend the entire day working with _____, _____, who has extensive
experiences working with _____. If you find this to be a worthwhile
experience, I can also arrange to have _____ visit you here at
_____ School.

Again, I stand ready to assist you in making this school year a successful experience.

Sincerely,

_____
Principal

cc: Specialist's Supervisor

(This letter can be easily adapted when it is sent by both coevaluators.)

Date

Name of Specialist and
Name of School

Dear _____:

I was pleased that your visit to _____ School was a worthwhile
professional development experience. I want to continue assisting you to improve your job
performance as a _____. Therefore, I have made arrangements for
_____, a _____ from _____ School, to
spend the entire school day with you on _____, _____, 00XX. During that time,
_____ will work with you in the following areas:

(List specific areas, e.g., planning, general organization.)

Again, I stand ready to assist you in making this school year a successful experience.

Sincerely,

_____

Principal

cc: Specialist's Supervisor

Sample Document 4.5
Letter Offering the Specialist Articles to Read
(Place on school letterhead)

(This letter can be easily adapted when it is sent by both coevaluators.)

Date

Name of Specialist and
Name of School

Dear _____:

In an effort to assist you to improve your performance as a _____, I
am providing the enclosed journal articles for you to read:

(List titles of articles.)

I stand ready to assist you in making this a successful school year.

Sincerely,

_____

Principal

Enclosures

cc: Specialist's Supervisor

Sample Document 4.6
Letter Referring the Specialist to a Specific Section in the Staff Handbook
or Other Reference Guide
(Place on school letterhead)

(This letter can be easily adapted when it is sent by both coevaluators.)

Date

Name of Specialist and
Name of School

Dear _____:

The _____ School Handbook is designed to provide information
relative to procedures that help ensure the smooth operation of our school. Because you had
difficulty in _____

_____

_____, a copy of sections on

_____ is enclosed. Please carefully
review these sections of the handbook to prevent this situation from occurring in the future:

_____ TOPIC _____   ___PAGE___

As always, I stand ready to assist you in making this a successful school year.

Sincerely,

_____

Principal

Enclosures

cc: Specialist's Supervisor

NOTE TO PRINCIPAL: When preparing the Unsatisfactory Evaluation Document, include a
copy of the pages cited in the handbook.

Sample Document 4.7
Letter Encouraging the Specialist to Attend Workshops or Classes
(Place on school letterhead)

(This letter can be easily adapted when it is sent by both coevaluators.)

Date

Name of Specialist and
Name of School

Dear _____:

The _____ Staff Bulletin lists several in-service
opportunities that may be beneficial in your efforts to improve your job performance as a
_____. These in-service classes appear to be related to the items that I
specified in the memorandum of concerns dated _____, 00XX. Therefore, I
recommend that you enroll in the following class(es):

       _____ <u>COURSE TITLE</u> _____   <u>PAGE/S IN BULLETIN</u>

I sincerely hope that these classes will help you improve your performance as a
_____ at _____ School. As always, I stand ready
to assist you in making this school year a successful experience. If you wish to discuss these
classes or other school issues, please see my secretary to set up a meeting with me.

Sincerely,

_____
Principal

Enclosures

cc: Specialist's Supervisor

NOTE TO PRINCIPAL: When preparing the Unsatisfactory Evaluation Document, include a
               copy of the pages from the in-service announcement.

Sample Document 4.8
Letter Encouraging the Specialist to Attend a Convention
(Place on school letterhead)

(This letter can be easily adapted when it is sent by both coevaluators.)

Date

Name of Specialist and
Name of School

Dear _____:

The _____ District Education Association Convention is scheduled

to be held from _____, _____, 00XX to _____, _____, 00XX, at the

_____.

The convention booklet lists several workshops that may assist you in improving your

performance as a _____ at _____ School. I

recommend that you attend the following workshops:

    <u>TITLE</u> <u>DATE</u>   <u>TIME</u>   <u>ROOM</u>

I believe this convention should be professionally rewarding. As always, I stand ready to assist

you in making this school year a successful experience.

Sincerely,

_____
Principal

cc: Specialist's Supervisor

(This letter can be easily adapted when it is sent by both coevaluators.)

Date

Name of Specialist and
Name of School

Dear _____:

This letter is a summary of our conference held in my office at _____, on _____, 00XX. I began the meeting by stating my concerns about your inability to effectively perform your duties and responsibilities as a _____ at _____ School. These concerns were as follows:

    1.

    2.

I also offered you the following immediate suggestions to improve your performance of your duties and responsibilities:

    1.

    2.

I want to continue supporting your efforts to improve your performance as a _____, and stand ready to assist you in this endeavor.

Sincerely,

_____
Principal

cc: Specialist's Supervisor

Sample Document 4.10
Letter Reviewing Assistance Provided to the Specialist
(Place on school letterhead)

(This letter can be easily adapted when it is sent by both coevaluators.)

Date

Name of Specialist and
Name of School

Dear _____:

During the past ___ weeks, I have made recommendations to improve your job performance as a _____ in the following areas:

- •
    - -
    - -
    - -
- •
    - -
    - -
- •
    - -
    - -
    - -

I would like to meet with you to further discuss the above suggestions for improvement as well as progress that you believe you are making to improve your performance as a _____.

As always, I stand ready to assist you in making this school year a successful experience.

Sincerely,

_____
Principal

cc: Specialist's Supervisor

Sample Document 4.11
Memorandum to the District Office Requesting Observation of and Assistance for the Specialist
(Place on school letterhead)

(This memorandum can be easily adapted when it is sent by both coevaluators.)

Date:

To: District Office Director or Department Head's Name

From: Principal's Name

Re: Request for Assistance

This is a request for assistance for _____, a _____ at _____ School. _____'s job performance has deteriorated to the degree that I am anticipating issuing an unsatisfactory evaluation if his/her performance does not improve.

_____ is having particular difficulty in the following areas:

Please contact me at _____ to finalize arrangements. Thank you for your assistance.

cc: Specialist's Supervisor

Date:

To: Principal's Supervisor's Name

From: Principal's Name

Re: Potential Unsatisfactory Evaluation

During September and October, 00XX, observations were made of all specialists assigned to

_____ School. Because of concerns about the performance of

_____, who is a _____, his/her supervisor,

_____, my assistant principal, _____, and I have conducted

observations of _____ performing his/her duties:

_____Day_____	____Date____	____Time_____	_____Observer_____

(List days, dates, times, and observers.)

These observations represent a reasonable sampling of his/her responsibilities and included
assignments in the morning and afternoon.

During follow-up conferences, _____'s strengths and limitations were discussed by
_____, _____ supervisor, and me. In addition, we offered
recommendations and set a reasonable period of time for necessary improvement.

Attached are copies of the conference summary letters and a memorandum of concerns listing
specific recommendations for improvement. Also enclosed are copies of the formal and informal
evaluation forms that were used to observe specialists.

_____ and I have followed the same procedures and used the same evaluation forms as outlined in a letter sent to all specialists on _____, 00XX. That letter explained the evaluation process at _____ School. I will inform you with regard to issuance of this potential unsatisfactory evaluation, and would like for you to review my documentation before it is finalized.

Enclosures

cc: Attorney for the School District
       Specialist's Supervisor

(This memorandum can be easily adapted when it is sent by both coevaluators.)

Date:

To: Specialist's Name

From: Principal's Name

Re: Accomplishment of Recommendations for Improvement

A memorandum relative to your role as a _____ was sent to you in a sealed envelope, marked "confidential," on _____, 00XX. The memorandum listed my concerns and recommendations for improving your performance as a _____. The memorandum was intended to provide you with clear directions to improve in your performance of your duties and responsibilities.

This is a follow-up to that memorandum and is designed to assess implementation of the recommendations that were made to improve your performance. The rating scale listed below provides an indicator to measure your attainment of the recommendations.

5 = Demonstrated an excellent level of accomplishment
4 = Demonstrated a satisfactory level of accomplishment
3 = Demonstrated a satisfactory level of accomplishment, but needs improvement
2 = Demonstrated a marginal level of accomplishment and needs substantial improvement
1 = Demonstrated an unsatisfactory level of accomplishment

Concern # 1

Recommendations

Attainment
of Recommendations

A.

_____

B.

_____

C.

_____

D.

_____

Comments

Concern # 2

Recommendations

Attainment
of Recommendations

A.

_____

B.

_____

C.

_____

D.

_____

Comments

Recommendations

Attainment
of Recommendations

A.   _____

B.   _____

C.   _____

D.   _____

Comments

Concern # 4

Recommendations

Attainment
of Recommendations

A.   _____

B.   _____

C.   _____

D.   _____

Comments

Although you have made some improvements, your overall performance has not improved since I sent my first memorandum of concerns to you. In fact, you are unable to successfully respond to and implement the recommendations that were made to improve your performance. Therefore, I want to clearly state that, if your performance does not improve within the next 30 school days, you will receive an unsatisfactory evaluation with a recommendation for dismissal from the school district.

_____, your supervisor, will continue to work with you to improve your performance. In addition, _____, assistant principal, will continue to conduct informal observations and offer you suggestions for improvements. As always, I will continue to conduct informal and formal observations to help you to improve your performance. Our primary purpose is to ensure that our students have a quality learning environment and that you have a successful school year.

If you have any questions about this memorandum, or if you disagree with my assessment of your performance, you must inform me in writing no later than November __, 00XX, or see my secretary to schedule a meeting with me to discuss this memorandum. At this meeting, you may have representation of your choice.

cc: Specialist's Supervisor

Sample Document 4.14
Cover Page for the Unsatisfactory Evaluation Documentation
(Place on school letterhead)

UNSATISFACTORY EVALUATION DOCUMENTATION

FOR

_____, (Title)

SUBMITTED BY

_____, PRINCIPAL

_____ SCHOOL

_____ SCHOOL DISTRICT

_____, 00XX

You must organize the unsatisfactory evaluation documentation using an organized format (such as the basic outline provided in the table of contents on the following page) and place it in a three-ring binder (two or more inches). This is one example of how the documentation can be organized. It is important that your documents and your presentation are in a logical sequence that is easy for you to present and for a hearing officer at any level to follow and understand.

This binder will serve as the master document. Then, before the initial unsatisfactory evaluation conference, make the additional copies that you will need. For example, the specialist's representative should receive a binder with all of the documentation--except your opening and closing statements and any personal notes you might have.

TABLE OF CONTENTS

I. Letters to Staff Members at the beginning of school
   A. Welcome Staff at the Beginning of the School Year
   B. Assigning a Buddy Staff Member

II. Identification of Evaluator
   A. Letter Identifying the Specialist's Evaluator
   B. School Roster for Specialist Signatures Acknowledging Receipt of Evaluation Letter

III. Evaluation Procedures for the School
   A. Memorandum Explaining the Evaluation Process
   B. Informal Observation Form
   C. Pre-Observation Conference Planning Form
   D. Formal Observation/Conference Summary Form
   E. Job Description for the Specialist
   F. Evaluation Section of the Specialist's Contract

IV. Observation Documentation

   A. Observation Forms
   B. Summary Letters of Conferences Following Observations of the Specialist
   C. Summaries of Monthly Observations of Staff Members

V. Identified Need for Improvement
   A. Memorandum of Concerns and Recommendations
   B. Memorandum of Accomplishments

VI. Letters/Documents Relative to Assistance Provided
   A. Observation of a Specialist in the Same School
   B. Visitation by the Specialist to Another School
   C. Visitation by a Specialist From Another School
   D. Articles to Read
   E. Section in the Staff Handbook
   F. Workshop to Attend
   G. Convention to Attend
   H. Request for Observation by a District Supervisor Related to the Intensive Assistance Plan
   I. Review of Assistance

VII. Parental Complaints
   A. Letters Informing the Specialist About Parental Complaints
   B. Parental Complaints Filed Against the Specialist

When you realize that a specialist might receive an unsatisfactory evaluation, you must collect background information to include in the documentation binder that you will to present at the various hearings. The Checklist for Collecting Historical Information About the Specialist includes basic historical information that you need.

CHECKLIST FOR COLLECTING HISTORICAL INFORMATION ABOUT THE SPECIALIST

_____SCHOOL

00XX-00XX

Specialist's Name_____

☐ Contact the personnel department to find out the specialist's current area of certification.

☐ Check the specialist's personnel file and read previous letters warning the specialist about unsatisfactory performance. Note the dates and the name(s) of the evaluator(s).

☐ Check the specialist's personnel file and read previous specialist evaluation documents. Carefully read for written comments about unsatisfactory job performance or warnings given by previous supervisors as well as comments providing recommendations for improvement. Note the dates and the name(s) of the evaluator(s).

☐ Check the local school file for any written warnings about an unsatisfactory evaluation. Note the dates and the name(s) of the evaluator(s).

☐ Check the local school records to find out the number of days the specialist has been absent and the number of times the specialist has been late to work as related to an unsatisfactory evaluation.

☐ Check the local school file for any misconduct charges against the specialist as related to an unsatisfactory evaluation.

☐ Contact the department responsible for workers' compensation to determine if the specialist has filed claims for workers' compensation as related to an unsatisfactory evaluation.

5 Implementing a Plan of Intensive Assistance

Don't be afraid to tell specialists what you want them to do.

Suggested Timeline: November

During September and October, you, as coevaluators, should have conducted informal and formal observations of all specialists to identify those who are experiencing difficulties performing their duties. If an assistant principal is available, he or she should have also conducted informal observations of the specialists and provided them with copies of the completed observation forms. For any specialist whose performance is unsatisfactory, you should have held meetings to discuss the specialist's performance and followed up with letters to the specialist summarizing the meetings.

If your efforts and the efforts of the coevaluator did not improve the specialist's performance, then move to the next step in the evaluation process. You and the coevaluator should have written a memorandum of concerns to the specialist listing specific concerns, specific examples of performance problems, and recommendations for improvement. Through the memorandum of concerns, you have given the specialist an opportunity to improve his or her performance. You and the coevaluator must now make an assessment to determine the degree to which those recommendations for improvement were implemented and send the specialist a memorandum of accomplishment (see Sample Document 4.13). If the specialist failed to implement the recommendations and did not achieve an acceptable level of performance, you should develop an intensive assistance plan (see Sample Documents 5.1 and 5.2). If your school district does not require a formal intensive assistance plan, you should use the memorandum of concerns and the memorandum of accomplishments to document the intensive assistance that you provided to meet the requirement for due process. To strengthen your documentation and to show that you attempted to help the specialist improve his or her performance, it is important that you provide some type of planned intensive assistance prior to taking formal job dismissal action.

An example of an intensive assistance plan is shown in Sample Document 5.1. This form would be appropriate for a specialist who works full-time at one school. It contains sections for background information, implementation expectations, concerns and recommendations, and consequences if performance does not improve. If a specialist works less than full-time at your school, a short version of an intensive assistance plan can be used (see Sample Document 5.2.)

Nevertheless, if your school district does require an intensive assistance plan, then you and the coevaluator must follow contractual procedures or state statutes that pertain to the implementation of an intensive assistance plan. This provision is usually included to ensure that the specialist is given written notification relative to the need for substantial improvement.

When you prepare the intensive assistance plan, you must specify the contractual provisions that govern the intensive assistance plan. For example, the plan usually includes your concerns about job performance and recommendations for improvement, a list of resources available in the school district to help the specialist, and the timeline to complete the intensive assistance plan. You must further state that, if the specialist does not improve, you will move to the dismissal stage of the evaluation process. Both coevaluators as well as the specialist should date and sign the intensive assistance plan. Do not be surprised, however, if the specialist refuses to sign and date the intensive assistance plan. In fact, the specialist may reject any support or assistance that either or both of you have offered. Therefore, it is important that you inform the specialist that he or she may have representation at the meeting.

During November, the following should occur:

❑ Prior to formal observations of specialists receiving intensive assistance, hold a preobservation conference and have the staff member discuss his or her plans and expected outcomes of the activity/event you will observe (see Sample Document 3.4).

❑ Conduct three formal observations and provide feedback listing areas of weakness and recommendations for improvement, and give a timeline of 3 weeks or more for necessary improvements (see Sample Document 4.10).

❑ If you are not using an intensive assistance plan, continue to write a memorandum of concerns listing recommendations following observations and hold a meeting to discuss the concerns (see Sample Document 4.1).

❑ Write a letter to the specialist summarizing the meeting held to discuss concerns and recommendations (see Sample Document 4.8).

❑ Continue conducting daily observations to identify specialists who may be experiencing problems and maintain the Summary of Observations of Staff Members (see Sample Document 3.5).

❑ Continue providing opportunities for the specialist to attend workshops conducted by the school district (see Sample Document 4.7).

❑ Continue offering the specialist articles to read that contain suggestions for improving his or her performance (see Sample Document 4.5).

❑ Issue a letter reviewing assistance provided to the specialist (see Sample Document 4.10).

❑ Send a potential unsatisfactory evaluation update letter to your supervisor (see Sample Document 4.12).

❑ Continue maintaining a parental complaint file (both verbal and written) for each staff member (see Sample Document 3.8).

❑ Continue to keep copies of all notes written to you by the specialist about his or her problems or other school-related issues.

❑ Maintain contact with the district's personnel department representative and attorney.

❑ Prior to making formal observations of staff members who are receiving intensive assistance, hold a preconference, and have the staff member explain specific plans for improvement and expected outcomes.

❑ Continue using the weekly school bulletin to provide information to document your attempt to provide assistance to the specialist.

❑ Continue recording each parental complaint on the standard complaint form and meet with the specialist about the situation. Then write a letter to the specialist stating your disposition on the parental complaint and forward it to the staff member for his or her response. File the complaint, your disposition letter, and any response from the specialist.

Administrative Tips to Remember

❑ Conduct at least three observations ranging from 30 minutes to one hour each.

❑ If possible, have an assistant principal conduct daily informal observations. Give the specialist a copy of the actual observation form (see Sample Document 3.2).

❑ If the staff member is improving, note the fact on the observation form, but re-emphasize recommendations for improvement that were stated previously.

INTENSIVE ASSISTANCE PLAN

_____ School District

Name of Staff Member   _____ Date   _____

Area(s) of Certification   _____ Work Site   _____

<u>Background Information</u>

Prior to this intensive assistance plan, _____, principal of _____ School, _____, the _____ supervisor, and _____, the assistant principal, conducted observations and made recommendations to improve the job performance of _____ during the 00XX-00XX school year. During September, October, and November 00XX, informal and formal observations were made of _____ in his/her role as the school _____. These observations represent a reasonable sampling and included _____'s morning and afternoon assignments. During the follow-up conferences, _____ and discussed _____'s strengths and limitations with him/her. The principal and the specialist's supervisor offered recommendations to _____ to help him/her to improve his/her job performance, provided him/her assistance, and set a reasonable time for improvement. In addition, _____ wrote and _____ received a written memorandum dated October __, 00XX, that outlined specific concerns and recommendations to improve job performance. Despite the opportunities for self-improvement, _____ did not attain an acceptable level of job performance. Then _____ sent a letter to the director of curriculum outlining specific concerns about _____ based on district's performance expectations for employees in the same position. As a result, _____ will be placed on an intensive assistance plan to improve his/her performance effective _____, _____, 00XX.

The purpose of the intensive assistance plan is to improve _____'s performance in the areas of _____. This intensive assistance plan is specifically designed to improve _____'s performance, specifically

_____.

Implementation of Intensive Assistance plan

This intensive assistance plan will begin on _____, _____ __, 00XX, and end on _____, 00XX. On _____, 00XX, _____ will meet with _____, the principal; _____, the specialist's supervisor; and _____, director of curriculum, to discuss the assistance plan to improve his/her performance as a _____.

_____'s failure or unwillingness to participate in this plan or to improve his/her job performance as specified in this plan may result in a recommendation that he/she be dismissed from the _____ School District.

Listed below are the concerns and recommendations to improve his/her performance:

Concern # 1
(State concern and give an example.)

Recommendations for Concern # 1

1. By _____, 00XX, Mr./Ms. _____ will....

2. Mr./Ms. _____ will....

3. Mr./Ms. _____ will....

4. Mr./Ms. _____ will.... *(Use as many recommendations as needed for concern #1.)*

5. By _____ 00XX, Mr./Ms. _____ will....

Concern # 2

(State concern and give an example.)

Recommendations for Concern # 2

1. By _____, 00XX, Mr./Ms. _____ will....

2. Mr./Ms. _____ will....

3. Mr./Ms. _____ will....

4. Mr./Ms. _____ will.... *(Use as many recommendations as needed for concern #2.)*

5. By _____ 00XX, Mr./Ms. _____ will....

Concern # 3

(State concern and give an example.)

Recommendations for Concern # 3

1. By _____, 00XX, Mr./Ms. _____ will....

2. Mr./Ms. _____ will....

3. Mr./Ms. _____ will....

4. Mr./Ms. _____ will.... *(Use as many recommendations as needed for concern #3.)*

5. By _____ 00XX, Mr./Ms. _____ will....

<u>Concern # 4</u>

(State concern and give an example.)

<u>Recommendations for Concern # 4</u>

1. By _____, 00XX, Mr./Ms. _____ will....

2. Mr./Ms. _____ will....

3. Mr./Ms. _____ will....

4. Mr./Ms. _____ will.... *(Use as many recommendations as needed for concern #4.)*

5. By _____ 00XX, Mr./Ms. _____ will....

<u>Concern # 5</u>

(State concern and give an example.)

<u>Recommendations for Concern # 5</u>

1. By _____, 00XX, Mr./Ms. _____ will....

2. Mr./Ms. _____ will....

3. Mr./Ms. _____ will....

4. Mr./Ms. _____ will.... *(Use as many recommendations as needed for concern #5.)*

5. By _____ 00XX, Mr./Ms. _____ will....

As agreed upon by the _____ School District in _____ 00XX, _____, principal of _____ School, and Director of Curriculum, will monitor the implementation of this intensive assistance plan with ongoing revisions and modifications as needed. At the end of the intensive assistance plan, they will meet by _____ __, 00XX, to review outcomes of the plan. By _____ __ __, 00XX, _____, principal; _____, supervisor; and _____, Director of Curriculum, will write the final report to formally notify _____ of their recommendation to return him/her to the established district evaluation process, to continue intensive assistance, or to end the intensive assistance because it was unsuccessful. In the latter instance, dismissal procedures would begin as specified in the master contract.

A copy of this intensive assistance plan and the final report will be sent to the specialist at the end of the plan and then be placed in the specialist's personnel file.

_____

Specialist's Signature   Date

_____

Principal's Signature   Date

_____

Supervisor's Signature   Date

_____

Director of Curriculum's Signature   Date

cc: Chief Personnel Director
      Specialist
      Specialist's Representative

INTENSIVE ASSISTANCE PLAN
_____ SCHOOL DISTRICT

Name _____ Date _____

Date Plan Initiated _____ Date Plan Completed_____

Assignment _____ School Site _____

I. List of Concerns

    A. _____

    B. _____

    C. _____

    D. _____

    E. _____

    F. _____

    G. _____

    H. _____

    I. _____

    J. _____

II. Specialist's Plan for Improvement

    A. _____

    B. _____

    C. _____

    D. _____

    E. _____

    F. _____

    G. _____

    H. _____

    I. _____

    J. _____

III. Plans to Assist Specialist

    A. _____

    B. _____

    C. _____

    D. _____

    E. _____

    F. _____

    G. _____

    H. _____

    I. _____

    J. _____

IV. Evaluator's Comments

    ____ • Has met the expectation and timelines of the intensive assistance plan.

    ____ • Has not met the expectation and timelines of the intensive assistance plan.

_____

_____

_____

_____

_____

V. Final Recommendations

    ____ • Recommend continuing employment, discontinuing intensive assistance.

    ____ • Recommend continuing employment, continuing intensive assistance.

    ____ • Recommend starting dismissal procedures.

Specialist's Signature _____ Date _____

Principal's Signature _____ Date _____

Supervisor's Signature_____ Date _____

Note to Specialist: Your signature acknowledges that you are aware of your intensive assistance plan. It does not mean that you concur with the plan.

cc: Chief Personnel Director
      Specialist
      Specialist's Representative

Sample Document 5.3
Letter Stating That Failure to Achieve a Satisfactory Level of Performance Will Result in an
Unsatisfactory Evaluation
(Place on school letterhead)

(This letter can be easily adapted when it is sent by both coevaluators.)

Date

Name of Specialist and
School Address

Dear _____:

From September through December of the 00XX-00XX school year, formal and informal
observations were made of you conducting your duties as the _____ at
_____ School. Specifically, observations were conducted on:

| ____Day____ | ____Date____ | ____Time____ | _____Observer_____ |

(List days, dates, times, and observers.)

These observations represent a reasonable sampling of your performance and included all aspects
of your assignment, both morning and afternoon.

In addition to memoranda that were sent to you outlining concerns, conferences were held with
you to discuss limitations, suggestions for improvement, and available assistance as well as a
reasonable time for necessary improvement. Letters summarizing our conferences were sent to
you on October __, November __, and December, 00XX.

Unfortunately, your performance has not improved to a satisfactory level. Therefore, this letter
serves as official notification that failure to achieve a satisfactory level of performance by
January __, 00XX, will result in the issuance of an unsatisfactory evaluation.

Sincerely,

_____

Principal

cc: Specialist's Supervisor

6 Deciding on Retention or Dismissal

Don't be afraid to make a decision to recommend the dismissal of a specialist who either won't do or can't do the job.

Suggested Timeline: December

You, as the principal, and the coevaluator must decide to recommend that the specialist continue in employment or be dismissed. The decision must be carefully made after conducting numerous observations; documenting concerns, as well as improvement, in memoranda sent to the specialist; collecting additional data; and holding meetings with the specialist, which should include his or her representative. If the decision is made to recommend dismissal, you and the coevaluator must begin preparing for the series of hearings specified in the specialist's contract, which usually includes a hearing before an impartial hearing officer. You must prove that the specialist is incompetent and should be recommended for dismissal from the school district.

Therefore, when preparing your documentation to substantiate that the specialist's performance is unsatisfactory, you and the coevaluator should not use flowery language to mask the incompetence of the specialist. If you overrate the specialist, it will backfire during the dismissal proceedings. For example, the specialist's representative or the third-party hearing officer can use your positive words to show that your evaluation of the specialist is misleading and that the allegations of incompetency lack support.

As you proceed with the hearings, the specialist and his or her representative may be antagonistic toward you and the coevaluator. Not only will the specialist and his or her representative deny that the specialist had any performance problems, but they will say that you and the coevaluator are destroying the specialist's excellent professional reputation. In fact, they may describe how the specialist has been a loyal employee for many years in the district and say that the specialist's personnel file contains excellent evaluations. To show that the specialist received average or above average evaluations before working under your supervision, the representative will probably bring to the conference copies of the specialist's evaluations completed by previous administrators. The specialist and his or her representative will blame you, the coevaluator, students in your school, and their parents. They never acknowledge that the specialist has performance problems.

Also, the specialist may write letters to school board members, the superintendent, or your supervisor to criticize you and your supposedly unfair evaluation tactics. Furthermore, the specialist may spread rumors about your unprofessional conduct in dealing with him or her. Moreover, the specialist may try to influence other staff members who may be concerned about their own evaluations. Nevertheless, you must continue the evaluation process despite these allegations. In fact, many of your staff members probably are already aware of the specialist's incompetence and are wondering what took you so long to take action. Most staff members may be silent on this issue; however, the vast majority will support your efforts to remove the incompetent specialist. Although you may be tempted to tell staff members about the incompetent specialist, you must keep personnel matters confidential and never discuss these problems with staff members, board members, parents, or other individuals.

The specialist's representative will also tell you and the coevaluator at a meeting that you have too much documentation and that you are out to "get" the specialist, or the specialist's representative may argue that you have too little documentation to support the unsatisfactory evaluation. The specialist or his or her representative will argue that you have not substantiated the unsatisfactory evaluation and, therefore, the case should be ended. Nevertheless, if the specialist's representative verbally attacks you instead of your documentation, you have probably done an excellent job in presenting your case. Despite the psychological game of the specialist's representative, you and the coevaluator must understand that the specialist's representative is doing his or her duty, which is to protect the specialist's job.

Remember that you must support each incompetency charge with firsthand documentation to prove an unsatisfactory evaluation. That is, you and the coevaluators should not use trivial reasons to dismiss the specialist. Moreover, you must be able to group the documentation with regard to the incompetency areas, so that an impartial third party can follow and easily understand. Furthermore, you must group letters, memoranda of concerns, and other documentation to show that you provided support to the specialist and gave him or her a chance to improve before you issued the incompetency charges. You and the coevaluators must categorize the alleged incompetency charges into specific areas, such as

- Failure to treat children equitably and free from bias
- Failure to maintain a safe environment for children with special needs
- Ineffective performance of the normal duties required of a competent specialist
- Neglecting to use proper disciplinary procedures
- Failure to maintain a harmonious and effective relationship; free of unwarranted dissension with parents, children, teachers, administrators, supervisors, or all of these
- Inability to cooperate with others with reference to substantial and serious matters, as well as with regard to unimportant and inconsequential affairs
- Causing dissension and lack of harmony among colleagues, parents, children, school administrators, supervisors, or all of these
- Failure to carry out recommendations provided in a memorandum of concerns from the administrator and the supervisor, failure to follow intensive improvement plan, or both
- Lacking sufficient knowledge in the specialist's area of responsibility
- Inability to explain the specialist's area of expertise
- Lack of rapport with children
- Insufficient communications with children, parents, and staff members
- Inappropriate use of time
- Failure to be punctual for appointments with children
- Failure to recognize and meet the needs of children
- Failure to accept recommendations from the school administrators, supervisors, or both
- Lack of self-direction
- Refusal to complete mandated reports
- Continual disregard for scheduled activities

After identifying the areas of incompetence, which become the charges, you should number them and list at least one example for each charge. For easy reference, you should develop a system to cross-reference the charges with the documentation that you submit. This will make your presentation easier.

During December, the following should occur:

❏ Continue conducting formal and informal observations and hold conferences as necessary (see Sample Documents 3.2 and 3.4).

❏ Review the documentation binder for grammatical or spelling errors; also be sure you use language that the third-party reader can follow and understand.

❏ Identify about five to eight incompetency charges to support your unsatisfactory evaluation of the specialist.

❏ Use district letter or forms to complete the unsatisfactory evaluation.

❏ Maintain contact with the district's personnel department representative and attorney.

Administrative Tips to Remember

- ❑ Use first-hand information to substantiate the unsatisfactory evaluation.
- ❑ Follow contractual procedures when carrying out the unsatisfactory evaluation process.

7 Following Through With the Dismissal Process

Always accept a resignation at the time it is given.

Suggested Timeline: January

During this step in the dismissal process, you must prepare for the school-level conference. You should hand deliver a confidential letter to the specialist informing him or her that you intend to issue an unsatisfactory evaluation. If you have an assistant principal, he or she should witness the delivery of the letter to the specialist noting the date and time the specialist received it. You should always consider issuing an unsatisfactory letter on a Friday afternoon or the day before a school break. Issuing an unsatisfactory letter at the beginning of the week may create tension and disrupt the remainder of the week because the specialist may try to garner support among his or her peers. The specialist may even show the unsatisfactory evaluation letter to other staff members or may post the letter in the teacher's lounge to evoke the fear in the minds of staff members that you will "go after them, too." The disgruntled specialist may spread rumors about you and your personal life, as well as talk about the unfairness of the evaluation process, to plant negative thoughts about your leadership ability and your misuse of authority through the evaluation process used to dismiss staff members.

Despite the temptation to tell your side of the story to staff members who may ask about the situation and reveal information about the specialist's performance problems, you and other coevaluators involved in the evaluation must remember that personnel issues are confidential. One innocent remark taken out of context can jeopardize the unsatisfactory evaluation case. Basically, the specialist being evaluated can talk, but you, as the evaluator, cannot counter any false statements the specialist might make. If his or her actions disrupt the educational process, however, you should take necessary action, which may include using the misconduct provision of the contract. For example, the specialist cannot use school time to collect statements of support from other staff members or students.

Although you may want to remove the specialist from his or her position before the case is heard at the board level, you must allow the specialist to continue to function in his or her position until a decision is rendered. Any change in job title, decrease in pay, or a reduction in authority will be presented by the specialist's representative as evidence that you violated evaluation procedures and that your actions clearly show that you "had it in" for the specialist. The unsatisfactory evaluation conference at the school level is usually conducted with the specialist and his or her representative. Subsequent hearings will occur particularly if the staff member disagrees with your evaluation and recommendation.

You should carefully plan for the conferences and hearings that will be held to discuss the unsatisfactory evaluation and ensure that contractual timelines are met. At the school-level conference you will conduct the meeting, present documentation, and listen to the specialist's response to the documentation. The specialist will probably, and should, bring a representative to the conference. At this conference, you, as the principal, will be the primary presenter and will call on the specialist's supervisor to present his or her testimony relative to observations and assistance. Also, if you have an assistant principal, he or she should be present to take notes. If the assistant principal also has provided documentation relative to observations and assistance, he or she may testify or respond to questions from the specialist's representative.

At the school-level conference and district-level hearing, you should not allow the use of tape recorders or video cameras. At the board-level hearing, however, a court reporter must be present to meet the due process that is required by law. Specifically, in addition to being given: notification of the charges, an opportunity for a hearing, adequate time to prepare a rebuttal to the charges, access to evidence and names of witnesses, a hearing before an impartial tribunal, representation by counsel, an opportunity to present evidence and witnesses, an opportunity to cross-examine adverse witnesses, a decision based on the evidence and findings of the hearing, the specialist must be provided access to a record of the hearing and an opportunity to appeal. The record of the hearing may include a court reporter transcript.

Because you should hold a meeting with the specialist and his or her representative, you must establish and maintain a formal, business-like atmosphere. Therefore, it is essential that you plan for the conference. First of all, you must set the location to ensure privacy, determine the seating arrangement, and select the best position that will enable you to control the conference. For example, you should sit at the head of the table or behind your desk. You should never sit between the specialist and his or her representative. You should have a copy of the specialist's contract on the desk in front of you for easy reference, if necessary, and also to visually reinforce that the conference is governed by the contract. Remember that you may not be able to anticipate everything that will happen during the conference. You can and should, however, try to anticipate certain things that could potentially throw you off course. For example, if the specialist brings more than one person to the conference (e.g., an attorney, a union representative, a relative) be prepared to have the specialist identify who will be his or her official representative before proceeding with the conference. Any other individuals can only observe. Another example might be the specialist and the specialist's representative trying to pass notes to each other during the conference. If it becomes excessive or disruptive, inform them that they may request a recess to communicate with each other. Do not allow verbal attacks, raised voices, or finger pointing. If you find yourself in such a combative situation, warn the specialist and the representative to conduct themselves in a professional manner or you will discontinue the conference. If the unacceptable conduct continues or the meeting becomes confrontational, you can recess the meeting for 10 to 20 minutes. After the recess, if the specialist's representative continues to act unprofessionally, stand up and announce that the meeting is adjourned.

In addition to the opening statement that you have prepared for presenting the actual documentation and the closing statement when you sum up your presentation, you will need to prepare a general greeting to open the conference and set a business-like atmosphere. The greeting should include a reference to the contractual provision for the conference, as well as the guidelines for the conference (see Sample Document 7.8). Both the general greeting and the opening statement may be read or used as a guide to present information, whichever is more comfortable. In either case, you should read through it several times before the actual conference to ensure that it flows easily. Also plan to give a documentation binder (2 or more inches in size) to the specialist and the specialist's representative after your opening statement. Keep in mind that you will need to present all evidence to substantiate the unsatisfactory evaluation at the first conference. New evidence may not be presented at subsequent hearings. Information from the time of the first conference to the next conference, however, may be entered when the hearing officer requests an update relative to improvement and assistance provided to the specialist.

If you have followed the steps and tips in this guide, you will be confident that your documentation is well organized and supports your evaluation of the specialist's job performance. You must remember to be confident, patient, thorough in your presentation, and respond to questions from the specialist's representative with facts and evidence that can be substantiated relative to job performance and its effect on students.

Depending on the volume of documentation, this conference might last 4 or more hours or might even need to be adjourned to continue at a later date. In the case of the latter, schedule the continuation conference as soon as possible. This conference may be lengthy. You should keep it moving, however, by focusing on specifics when necessary and by summarizing or highlighting whenever possible.

It is important at the first conference to thoroughly go through the documentation and to verify that the specialist received copies of all documents that are being presented. If the representative objects to the inclusion of a document, say "I have noted your objection" and move on. It is better to leave documentation in than to take it out prematurely in the process. At a subsequent conference, the hearing officer might rule to remove the document.

You must be prepared for potential criticism on the part of the specialist and his or her representative, who may accuse you of failing to provide assistance, point out spelling and grammatical errors in documentation, say that you are a poor example of a principal, accuse you of favoritism of some staff members, and accuse you of exhibiting biases based on gender, race, religion, or age. No matter how frustrated or irritated you may become when the specialist and his or her representative make these accusations, do not become defensive in your responses or exhibit facial signs that reflect your irritation. The specialist's representative will design his or her cross-examination and rebuttal to challenge your decision and to cause doubt relative to your proceeding with a recommendation for dismissal.

Always expect the unexpected. And remember that, regardless of the degree of preparation, you may not be able to anticipate everything. Therefore, expect the unexpected and remain calm if something arises that you did not anticipate. If necessary adjourn the conference for a few minutes to determine what to do or to get an answer to a question. You might make arrangements before the conference to have an adviser (attorney for the district or your supervisor) on stand-by should you need on-the-spot consultation.

During the evaluation hearings, you may feel that you are "on trial" instead of the incompetent specialist. The specialist's representative may use confrontational strategies to frustrate you. You may be accused of showing favoritism, treating staff members differently based on race and gender, failing to clarify the roles and responsibilities, or all of these. The specialist or the specialist's representative may further charge that you

- Failed to follow state law or board policy when issuing this unsatisfactory evaluation
- Did not follow the master contract to evaluate the specialist
- Did not provide oral or written communication listing specific shortcomings and recommendations for improvement
- Harassed the specialist by conducting excessive observations
- Singled out this specialist from other specialists
- Have a vendetta against the specialist
- Have overstated the problem
- Are not qualified to conduct this evaluation because of your certification

The specialist will make every attempt to embarrass you to thwart the dismissal. Therefore, you should avoid social relationships with specialists or any staff members. Furthermore, you must never become romantically involved with a specialist or another staff member. Not only would such rumors be likely to surface during the evaluation process, but during the dismissal hearings, they might explode in the media.

Regardless of accusations that are made about how you conducted the specialist's performance evaluation, you must not show your anger or frustration. Raising your voice and shouting at the specialist and his or her representative will only encourage them to intensify their cross-examination and to continue making false accusations. Despite the fact that you will be under stress during the hearing, you must demonstrate poise, grace, and professionalism.

If you have followed the procedures outlined in this guide, your decision will probably not change. Therefore, at the conclusion of the conference, the specialist's representative may tell you that he or she needs to talk with his or her client before making a decision to proceed to the next level. On the other hand, he or she may tell you to go ahead and schedule the district-level conference. It is important to follow any contractual timeline for your school district. If the specialist's representative states that the specialist plans to retire or resign, you will need to work with the personnel department to secure a written statement that meets district requirements and that the timeline does not lapse before the retirement or resignation is formally submitted.

During January, the following should occur:

- ❏ Continue conducting formal and informal observations and hold conferences as necessary (see Sample Documents 3.2 and 3.4).

- ❏ Draft the letter of intent to issue an unsatisfactory evaluation and hand deliver it to the specialist with a copy to his or her representative (see Sample Document 7.1).

- ❏ Prepare the opening and closing statements for the unsatisfactory evaluation meeting and include reference to due process (see Sample Documents 7.2 and 7.3).

- ❏ Review the unsatisfactory evaluation binder to ensure that all appropriate documentation is included.

- ❏ Maintain contact with the district's personnel department representative and the attorney for the school district.

- ❏ Meet with your supervisor to discuss the unsatisfactory evaluation documentation.

- ❏ Send a letter to the staff member reminding him or her about the date, time, and location of the meeting (see Sample Document 7.4).

- ❏ Write the unsatisfactory evaluation using the established form for your district and write a letter to accompany the evaluation form informing the specialist of his or her right to review and respond to the evaluation (see Sample Documents 7.5 and 7.6).

- ❏ Prepare additional copies of the unsatisfactory evaluation binder (one for the specialist's representative and one for each coevaluator). Additional copies will be needed for the hearing officers of any subsequent hearings.

Administrative Tips to Remember

- ❑ **Hand deliver** the letter of intent to issue the unsatisfactory evaluation on a Friday afternoon.

- ❑ **Hand deliver** the letter scheduling the meeting after school the following week.

- ❑ Practice presenting your opening statement for the first hearing. Because the opening statement is from your personal notes, you do not have to share them with the specialist.

- ❑ Review strategies to ensure that you remain in control of the meeting and are not intimidated by the staff member's representative.

- ❑ Have an assistant principal or the supervisor who has participated in the evaluation process attend the hearing to take notes.

- ❑ Be prepared to respond to questions or criticisms regarding how the evaluation process was conducted.

- ❑ Do not get into a verbal confrontation with the specialist or his or her representative.

(This letter can be easily adapted when it is sent by both coevaluators.)

Date

Name of Specialist and
School Address

Dear_____:

This letter is to inform you that an unsatisfactory evaluation of your performance as a
_____ will be submitted to the personnel department.

A copy of your unsatisfactory evaluation will be given to you on _____,
_____, 00XX, at _____ in my office. The Master Contract, Section __ on pages
_____, will govern the procedures to ensure your due process during the evaluation hearings. If
you wish, you may be represented by a member of your bargaining unit or a person of your
choice.

After receiving the evaluation form, you will have __ hours to review my comments and respond
to them in writing if you wish. A copy of your response will be attached to the unsatisfactory
evaluation form before it is submitted to the personnel department with a recommendation for
your dismissal from the _____ School District.

Sincerely,

_____

Principal

cc: Specialist's Supervisor

Sample Document 7.2
Opening Statement for the Unsatisfactory Evaluation Conference

---

An unsatisfactory evaluation is issued when a staff member fails to respond to the efforts that were made to help improve his/her job performance and his/her failure to

_____.

When this occurs, there is a negative impact on students.

Prior to issuance of the unsatisfactory evaluation, contractual procedures were followed to ensure that procedural and substantive due process are applied. Section _____, Paragraph ___ on page ___ of the contract identifies the steps which are required by the _____ School District.

Since _____, _____ has been a _____ in the _____ School District and worked at _____ and _____ Schools. He/She was evaluated by _____ during the 00XX-00XX school year and by _____ during the 00XX-00XX school year. Both of his/her supervisors found his/her job performance skills to be below average. During those assignments in ___ different schools, he/she was unable to obtain and maintain a level of acceptable performance as a _____.

_____ is licensed in _____ and holds certification to work in the capacity of _____ at the _____ grade levels.

The following letters regarding his/her unsatisfactory job performance are on file in _____'s employee file in the department of personnel:

   Date   Principal   Summary of Statements Regarding Performance

NOTE: This statement should not be included in the Unsatisfactory Evaluation Document. It should be read at the beginning of each hearing.

In addition, the following unsatisfactory evaluations warning him/her about his/her unsatisfactory job performance are on file in _____'s employee file in the personnel department:

<u>Date</u>	<u>Principal</u>	<u>Summary of Statements Regarding Performance</u>

Listed below is a summary of _____'s absenteeism during the past three school years:

<u>Year</u>	<u>Number of Day Absent</u>	<u>Percent of Time Absent Per School Year</u>

00XX-00XX

00XX-00XX

00XX-00XX

(To Current Year)

On _____ different occasions, _____ filed for workers' compensation related to his job performance:

<u>Year</u>	<u>Claim</u>	<u>Disposition</u>

During his/her assignment at _____ School, he/she has:

- been absent _____ times for a total of _____ hours

<u>Dates</u> <u>Number of Hours</u>	<u>Reasons</u>

- been late to work _____ times for a total of _____ hours

<u>Dates</u>	<u>Number of Hours</u>	<u>Reasons</u>

- been charged with the following actions of misconduct related to his/her performance as a _____

<u>Date</u>	<u>Charge</u>	<u>Disposition</u>

Parents have also called the principal and written letters expressing concerns about the services provided by _____'.

As we proceed, I want to emphasize that contractual procedures and due process have been followed:

- The evaluation process was consistently applied. I informed all staff members about district and school expectations. In addition, the district-approved evaluation was made known to all staff members at _____ School. _____ was not singled out and the same standards were applied to all specialists.

- The _____ supervisor, the director of _____, the assistant principal at _____ School, and I conducted observations of _____'s job performance. These observations included all phases of his assignments as a guidance counselor.

- A continuous and accurately dated file of all observations and evaluations was maintained.

- _____ received written memoranda of concerns specifying the exact nature of the performance limitations.

- In each written memorandum of concern, _____ received specific suggestions for correcting these limitations and how to achieve a satisfactory level of performance.

- _____ was given a reasonable period of time for necessary improvements.

- _____ was informed that failure to achieve and maintain an acceptable level of performance by _____ would result in the issuance of an unsatisfactory evaluation.

Despite the opportunities that were provided for _____ to improve prior to the issuance of this unsatisfactory evaluation, _____ did not attain or maintain an acceptable level of performance.

At this point, I will review the documentation to support the issuance of this unsatisfactory evaluation.

Sample Document 7.3
Closing Statement for the Unsatisfactory Evaluation Conference

---

Unfortunately, _____'s overall performance as a
_____ has resulted in ineffective services provided to students, especially special needs students. His/Her failure to respond to the efforts that were made to help improve his/her job performance and his/her failure to _____ are justifications for issuing an unsatisfactory evaluation.

Therefore, I am recommending that _____ be relieved of his/her _____ responsibilities at _____ School and that he/she be dismissed from the _____ School District.

NOTE: This statement should not be included in the Unsatisfactory Specialist Evaluation
Document. It should be read at the end of each hearing.

Sample Document 7.4
Letter Reminding the Specialist About the Conference
(Place on school letterhead)

(This letter can be easily adapted when it is sent by both coevaluators.)

Date

Name of Specialist and
School Address

Dear _____:

This letter is to remind you about our meeting which has been scheduled for _____, January __, 00XX at _____ p.m. in my office to discuss the issuance of an unsatisfactory evaluation to you.

If you wish, you may be represented by a bargaining unit representative or anyone of your choice.

Sincerely,

_____
Principal

cc: Specialist's Supervisor

PERFORMANCE EVALUATION FORM

NAME_____ TITLE_____

SCHOOL_____ EVALUATION PERIOD_____

(Directions to evaluators: Use the space provided to summarize your appraisal of the performance of the staff member. If necessary, additional pages may attached.)

Percent of class time lost due to absences ____   Percent of class time lost due to tardiness ____

Evaluator(s) Rating   ☐ Excellent   ☐ Satisfactory   ☐ Marginal   ☐ Unsatisfactory

Evaluator's Signature	Title	Date
Evaluator's Signature (If coevaluated)	Title	Date

(Directions to staff member: After reading your performance evaluation, check indicating that you agree or disagree with your evaluator(s) statements and rating. Then sign on the lines below. Your signature only means that you have read this evaluation.)

☐ Agree   ☐ Disagree

Staff Member's Signature	Title	Date

(This letter can easily be adapted when it is sent by both coevaluators.)

Date

Name of Specialist and
School Address

Dear _____:

Enclosed is your performance evaluation for the 00XX-00XX school year. If you wish to respond in writing to this evaluation, you may attach your comments and submit them along with the evaluation form within _____ school days. The unsatisfactory evaluation and any comments will then be filed with the personnel department.

If you wish to meet relative to your evaluation, please contact my secretary to schedule a conference. At this meeting, you are entitled to have representative of your choice.

Sincerely,

_____

Principal

cc: Specialist's Supervisor

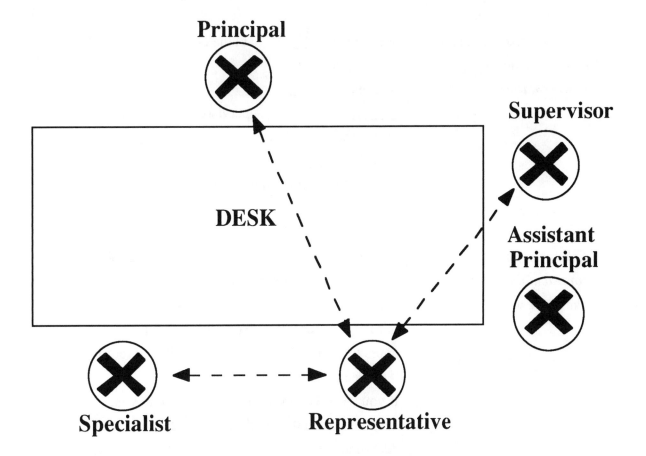

The above seating chart shows one possible arrangement for the school level hearing. As the principal, you are in charge of the hearing. Therefore, you must clarify procedures, set basic ground rules and explain the sequence of the hearing. You should formally greet the specialist and the specialist's representative, and introduce the specialist's supervisor and the assistant principal in attendance at the conference. The role of the assistant principal is to take notes of the meeting. He or she does not play an active role in this conference. You should have a copy of the master contract on the table or desk in front of you and refer to the section of the contract that governs the evaluation process. The dotted lines and arrows represent the flow of communication that should occur during the conference. The primary speakers are the principal, the specialist's representative, and the supervisor. The assistant principal may make a pertinent statement relative to his or her role in any observations and assistance provided to the specialist as well as respond to any questions from the specialist's representative. The specialist's representative may do all of the talking for the specialist, or may ask the specialist to respond to questions or make a statement.

Greeting

"Good afternoon, Mr./Ms. _____."

Introductions if you do not know the teacher representative

My name is _____. I am the principal of _____ School.

Mr./Ms. _____ is the _____ supervisor who has also worked with Mr./Ms. _____.

Mr./Ms. _____, assistant principal will sit in on the conference to take notes.

Acknowledgment of contractual provision and due process

"As I stated in my letter to you, the meeting today is to issue an unsatisfactory evaluation in accordance with Section ____, Paragraph _____ of the master contract. You will be given ____ hours to review the evaluation, sign it, and return it to me no later than _____.

If you wish, you may attach a response to your evaluation, and they will be sent to the personnel department.

Sequence of testimony	"As we proceed, I will present documentation to support the unsatisfactory evaluation. I would like to proceed without interruptions and will also call upon Mr./Ms._____ to provide documentation relative to his/her observations, support, assessment of Mr./Ms._____'s performance. After we have finished, Mr./Ms. _____, you and your representative will have an opportunity to examine the documentation and provide testimony."
Clarification of procedure	"Do you have any questions about the procedures for this conference? Let's proceed with the conference."

Remember that, if the specialist brings more than one person to the conference, you should ask the specialist to identify one person to serve as his or her official representative before proceeding with the meeting. Any other individuals can only observe. Do not allow notes to be passed between the specialist or others attending the meeting. Most important, do not allow audio or video taping of the conference.

Preparing for the Third-Party Hearing and Bringing Closure to the Evaluation Process

Be prepared to compromise on issues.

Suggested Timeline: February Through June

One of the most challenging steps in the process of handling an unsatisfactory evaluation involves presenting your case at a third-party hearing, which will determine if your documentation substantiates the recommendation for dismissal. After you send the specialist the initial letter that schedules the district-level conference (see Sample Document 8.1), all subsequent letters to the specialist will be sent from the personnel department, superintendent, or Board of Education. From February through June, you should be preparing for and presenting at hearings to bring closure to the unsatisfactory evaluation of the specialist. In addition, you will be bringing closure to the evaluation process for other staff members at your school.

Due process must be provided to the staff member by giving the specialist an opportunity to present his or her side of the case to a third party who is unfamiliar with the situation. Ideally, the hearings will be held in a timely fashion, but delays can occur for various reasons (e.g., scheduling problems, a change in the specialist's representative). The specialist might decide to take a medical leave. If this occurs, your personnel director must write a letter to the specialist informing him or her that the unsatisfactory evaluation process will resume when he or she returns to work from the medical leave. Although procedures in this guide follow a specific timeline (February for the district-level conference and March for the board-level hearing), you should adjust your schedule to adhere to the individual circumstances and guidelines for your district.

Just as you prepared for your school-level conference, you must plan for the district-level hearing. At the district level, individuals who hear the unsatisfactory evaluation case will assume an impartial position and will not have a copy of the unsatisfactory evaluation binder containing your documentation or specific knowledge about the case. Rather, you will present this documentation to the impartial hearing officer at the time of the hearing. Moreover, you must be prepared to present your evidence in a logical sequence to focus on key points that will help support each charge of incompetency.

The diagram in Sample Document 8.2 shows the usual seating arrangement for the district-level hearing. The hearing officer in charge of the conference will make an opening statement, usually explaining how the hearing will proceed, and giving the guidelines. Also, remember to address your comments to the hearing officer and not to the specialist or the specialist's representative, even if the specialist's representative asks you questions. Your task is to convince the hearing officer that the specialist is incompetent, not the specialist or his or her representative. Keep in mind, too, that your body language should show that you are calm and self-assured. You must also be emotionally prepared for the conference because you will again be subject to attack by the specialist's representative. In fact, that person may accuse you of being biased, giving no support to the specialist, being incompetent yourself, and so forth.

Notice that the specialist and his or her representative(s) are seated on one side, you and the coevaluator(s) are sitting on the opposite side, and the hearing officer is seated at the head of the conference table. If additional people are in the room, they should sit closest to the side with which they are associated.

Following the district-level conference, the hearing officer will send a letter to the specialist stating his or her decision to either uphold your recommendation for dismissal (see Sample Document 8.1) or deny that recommendation (see Sample Document 8.2). Depending on your school district, the superintendent may also send a letter of concurrence (see Sample Document 8.5). If the hearing officer upholds the recommendation for dismissal, it is likely that contractual provisions include an appeal at the school-board level. When the board-level hearing is scheduled, a letter will be sent to the specialist (see Sample Document 8.6).

At the board level, your responsibility will be to present your documentation and to testify at the board hearing. At this point, the board's attorney generally assumes the responsibility for presenting the case. Needless to say, this hearing undoubtedly will be quite stressful for you. You will again feel as if you are on trial. But, as stated previously with regard to the district-level conference, if you have followed the steps laid out in the previous chapters, you can feel confident that the hearing officer will recognize that you met the just-cause requirements and provided the specialist with adequate support and time for improvement. Once again, there is no guarantee that you will win. But, you will have taken action on behalf of the children in your school to remove an incompetent specialist.

The diagram in Sample Document 8.7 shows a general seating arrangement for a board-level hearing. Notice that the specialist and his or her representative(s) are seated on one side and that you and the coevaluators are seated across from the board panel. The board chairperson is in control of the hearing and will primarily communicate with the attorney for the district and with the specialist's representative or attorney. Again, direct your comments to the board chairperson or individual board members when they ask a question.

Even though preparing for an unsatisfactory evaluation of any staff member will take a great deal of your time, other duties will still require your attention. For example, the evaluation process for your other staff members must continue. Also, you must continue to observe and meet with the specialist who is receiving the unsatisfactory evaluation, and provide assistance to him or her. You should collect any new documentation, maintain it in a separate folder, and then present it to the hearing officer when the opportunity arises. The hearing officer may inquire if the specialist has shown any improvement since the school-level conference. If, however, the hearing officer does not ask, you should make reference during your closing statement to the fact that you are continuing your observations and providing assistance.

During February, the following should occur:

- ❏ Maintain contact with the district's personnel department representative and the attorney for the school district.
- ❏ Prepare to present at the district-level hearing the documentation for the unsatisfactory evaluation.
- ❏ Continue conducting formal and informal observations and holding conferences, as necessary (see Sample Documents 3.2 and 3.4).
- ❏ Continue providing tips to staff members in the weekly staff bulletin.

During March, the following should occur:

- ❏ Maintain contact with the personnel department and the attorney for the school district.
- ❏ Prepare to present the unsatisfactory evaluation documentation at the board level.
- ❏ Prior to formal observations of the staff member who is receiving intensive assistance, hold a preconference and have that person explain specific plans for improvement and expected outcomes.
- ❏ Continue conducting formal and informal observations and holding conferences as necessary (see Sample Documents 3.2 and 3.4).
- ❏ Begin completing the evaluations for all other staff members.
- ❏ Continue providing tips for staff members in the weekly staff bulletin.

During April, the following should occur:

- ❏ Begin preparing to close out the school year.

❑ Continue providing tips for staff members in the weekly staff bulletin.
❑ Finalize evaluation documentation of staff members.
❑ Follow contractual guidelines for informing staff members about procedures for completing their evaluations.

During the final step in the evaluation process, other specialists may request a conference to discuss their evaluation even though they have performed satisfactorily. You should meet individually with such specialists to discuss their evaluations. If you hold a conference, modify the seating arrangement because a more positive atmosphere will undoubtedly exist. But, you only hold such a conference if the specialist requests it. Still, general tips for holding a conference apply. For example, keep the following tips in mind:

❑ Schedule the conference to meet within the contractual timeline.
❑ Plan the seating arrangement so that you are not sitting next to the specialist.
❑ Provide as much privacy as possible.
❑ Extend a greeting and be cordial and relaxed, but maintain a businesslike atmosphere.
❑ Do not conduct a conference if you are upset or ill.
❑ Prepare notes to cover important items.
❑ Use facts and evidence related to job performance and its effect on students.
❑ Use well-organized documentation to support your evaluation of the staff member's performance on the job.
❑ Respond to questions from the staff member with facts that can be substantiated.
❑ Close the conference by highlighting the positive aspects of the staff member's job performance and, if necessary, comment on areas for improvement and state your commitment to providing support and resources to the specialist.

All evaluations of specialists, as well as those of other staff members, should be finalized and submitted to the personnel department following district guidelines. In addition you should reflect on the evaluation process itself and makes notes relative to how you can personally improve the implementation of the steps in your school.

While the information is still fresh in your mind, complete general assessments relative to the process. Such assessments may include summarizing the strengths and weaknesses of staff members for the purpose of identifying "buddy" staff members next year and formulating a plan for staff development. This step brings closure to the evaluation process for the school year, provides preliminary preparations for the next year, and reinforces the fact that the process is cyclical.

During May and June, the following should occur:

❑ Meet individually with staff members who request further clarification of their strengths, and make recommendations for improvement if necessary.

❑ Complete the appropriate district forms for all staff members who are identified as being scheduled for annual evaluations.

❑ Photocopy the completed evaluation forms for the local school files; then forward the original to the district personnel department.

❑ Issue the bulletin for closure of the school year.

❑ Send a letter to "buddy" staff members thanking them for providing support to new staff members (see Sample Document 8.10).

❑ Review the evaluation process and modify procedures and materials as needed for the next school year.

Sample Document 8.1
Letter Scheduling the District-Level Conference
(Place on school letterhead)

(This letter can be easily adapted when it is sent by both coevaluators.)

Date

Name of Specialist and
Name of School

Dear _____:

On _____, _____, a conference was held in my office with regard to an unsatisfactory evaluation that was issued to you. As a result of our meeting, you disagreed with the unsatisfactory evaluation and the recommendation that you be dismissed from the school district. As a result, a conference is scheduled with an impartial hearing officer at the District Administration Office in Room _____ at _____ a.m./p.m. on _____, _____, 00XX At this conference, you may be represented by a person of your choice.

Sincerely,

_____

Principal

cc: Specialist's Supervisor
       Specialist's Representative
       Principal's Supervisor
       Chief Personnel Director
       District Level Hearing Officer

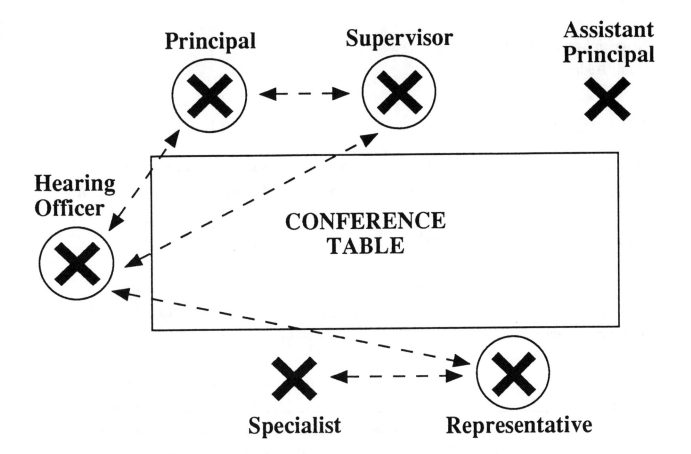

The above seating arrangement may be used for a conference on an unsatisfactory evaluation that is held before an impartial hearing officer. The hearing officer who is in charge of this hearing makes an opening statement, usually explaining how the hearing will proceed and giving the guidelines. Both sides present to the hearing officer. First, the principal presents for the administration, and the specialist's representative presents for the specialist. When you make your presentation to the hearing officer, always speak directly to him or her. Your goal is to convince the hearing officer that your documentation will substantiate the unsatisfactory evaluation. You are not trying to convince the specialist and his or her representative of the specialist's incompetence. Rather, you must convince the hearing officer -- who has had no involvement in the case -- that the specialist is incompetent. Therefore, you must take your time to carefully explain your documentation to the hearing officer. As you speak to the hearing officer, you must make eye contact with him or her. Try not to allow the specialist and his or her representative to distract you. They may not be looking at you during your presentation. Instead, they will probably be looking at the hearing officer or taking notes on your presentation. The arrows show the general flow of discussion. The hearing officer may ask questions of the specialist and/or the specialist's supervisor.

Sample Document 8.3
Letter From the District-Level Hearing Officer Informing the Specialist That He
or She Upholds the Recommendation for Nonrenewal or Dismissal
(Place on district letterhead)

Date

Name of Specialist and
Home Address

Dear _____:

In accordance with Section __, Paragraph __ of the master contract, a meeting was held on
_____ _____, 00XX, at ___ in Room ____ of the District Office Building. Also
present at the meeting were _____, principal; _____,
_____ supervisor; and _____, your representative.

_____ presented documentation and testimony relative to your
performance as a _____. _____ also presented
testimony in support of _____ assessment of your performance.

_____, your representative, presented testimony on your behalf and
stated _____. He/she said that you were not
provided with the assistance that you believed was necessary to help you fulfill your duties at
_____ School. _____ countered _____'s
statements in which he/she recommend your dismissal from the _____
School District and requested that you be transferred to another school.

After carefully reviewing the testimony and documentation, I believe there is sufficient evidence
to substantiate the unsatisfactory evaluation. Therefore, I am recommending to the
Superintendent that you be dismissed from the _____ school district.

During the remainder of this school year, you are expected continue in your position at
_____ School and fulfill all duties that have been assigned to you.

Sincerely,

District Level Hearing Officer

cc: Specialist's Supervisor
       Specialist's Representative
       Principal's Supervisor
       Chief Personnel Director
       Director of Compensation
       School Principal

Sample Document 8.4
Letter From the District-Level Hearing Officer Informing the Specialist That He or She
Does Not Uphold the Recommendation for Nonrenewal or Dismissal
(Place on district letterhead)

Date

Name of Specialist and
Home Address

Dear _____:

In accordance with Section __, Paragraph __ of the master contract, a meeting was held on
_____ _____, 00XX, at ___ in Room ____ of the District Administration
Building. Also present at the meeting were _____, principal;
_____, _____ supervisor; and _____,
your representative.

_____ presented documentation and testimony relative to your
performance as a _____. _____ also presented
testimony in support of _____ assessment of your performance.

_____, your representative, presented testimony on your behalf and
stated that you were not provided with the assistance that you believed was necessary to help you
fulfill your duties at _____ School.

After carefully reviewing the testimony and documentation that was presented, I believe that
there is insufficient evidence to substantiate the unsatisfactory evaluation. Therefore, you will
receive a revised evaluation indicating that your performance is satisfactory.

Sincerely,

District Level Hearing Officer

cc: Specialist's Supervisor
      Specialist's Representative
      Principal's Supervisor
      Chief Personnel Director

Sample Document 8.5
Letter From the Superintendent Concurring
With the Recommendation of the District Level-Hearing Officer
(Place on district letterhead)

Date

Name of Specialist and
Home Address

Dear _____:

This letter is to inform you that I concur with the recommendation of the chief personnel director that you be dismissed from the _____ School District. I am presenting a recommendation for your dismissal to the Board of Education. According to Section ___ Paragraph __ of the master contract you have a right to request a hearing at the Board level.

If you choose to request a hearing with the Board of Education, you will have a right to decide whether the meeting will be open or closed to the public, to cross-examine witnesses, and to present evidence on your own behalf. A court reporter will record the proceedings.

You are also entitled to be represented by the _____ Association or legal counsel of your choice to ensure that due process is followed according to the master contract.

Sincerely,

Superintendent of Schools

cc: Specialist's Supervisor
    Specialist's Representative
    Principal's Supervisor
    Chief Personnel Director
    Director of Compensation
    School Principal

Date

Name of Specialist and
Home Address

Dear _____:

At your request, a hearing has been scheduled with the Board of Education on _____,
_____ 00XX, at _____ p.m. in the Board Conference Room (Room 139) with
regard to the recommendation for your dismissal from the _____ School District.

Sincerely,

Secretary to the Board

cc: Specialist's Supervisor
     Specialist's Representative
     Principal's Supervisor
     Chief Personnel Director
     Compensation Director
     School Principal

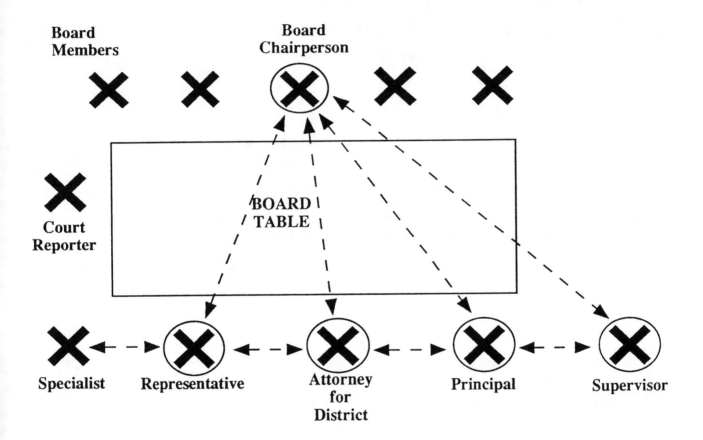

The diagram above shows a general seating arrangement for a Board hearing. Notice that the specialist and his or her representative(s) are seated on one side and that the coevaluators are seated across from the Board panel. The Board chairperson is in control of the hearing and will communicate primarily with the attorney for the district and with the specialist's representative or attorney. Direct your presentation to and respond to any questions from the Board chairperson or individual Board members.

Sample Document 8.8
Letter to the Specialist Stating That the Board Did Not Concur
With the Recommendation for Nonrenewal or Dismissal
(Place on district letterhead.)

Date

Name of Specialist and
Home Address

Dear _____:

The superintendent of schools made a recommendation to dismiss you from the
_____ School District; however, the Board of Education did not uphold this
recommendation. Therefore, you will return to your position as a _____ at
_____ school for the 00XX-00XX school year. All documentation with
regard to your unsatisfactory evaluation will be destroyed. In addition, your personnel file will
be cleared of any letters about this unsatisfactory evaluation. You are to resume your normal
duties as _____ at _____ School on
_____, _____, 00XX, at _____.

Sincerely,

President of the Board

cc: Specialist's Supervisor
      Specialist's Representative
      Principal's Supervisor
      Chief Personnel Director
      Director of Compensation
      School Principal

Date

Name of Specialist and
Home Address

Dear _____:

This letter is to inform you that based upon the evidence and testimony presented at the hearing conducted on _____, _____ 00XX, the Board of Education concurs with the Superintendent's recommendation to dismiss you from the _____ School District.

Please contact _____, Director of Compensation, at _____ for advisement with regard to payroll and fringe benefits. Your last day of employment with the _____ School District is _____, _____, 00XX.

You are expected to remove your personal effects from the classroom and to return any keys and/or other school property to _____, principal, at _____ School. If you do not remove your personal effects by _____, _____, 00XX, they will be donated to a community charitable organization.

Sincerely,

Chief Personnel Director

cc: Principal
        Director of Compensation
        Attorney for the School District
        Specialist's Representative

Date

Name of Staff member and
School Address

Dear _____:

Thank you for serving as a "buddy" staff member to a new staff member at
_____ School this school year. Sharing your ideas and expertise has helped
to make this a rewarding and successful experience for _____.

Enclosed is a certificate of appreciation for your contributions as a mentor. I hope this certificate
will serve as a lasting memento of your mentorship.

Again, my deepest appreciation for assisting _____ this school year.

Sincerely,

_____

Principal

Resource A:
Calendar With Suggested Timeline
of Actions for the Specialist's Evaluators

Two documents are provided in this section. The diagram shows the relationship among the specialist's evaluators, and the school year calendar shows the sequence of actions that should be taken by the evaluators during the unsatisfactory evaluation process. The calendar may be modified to fit individual situations as well as differences in district guidelines.

SCHEMATIC VIEW OF THE RELATIONSHIP AMONG THE SPECIALIST'S EVALUATORS

The diagram below shows a schematic view of the relationship among the specialist's evaluators. The actual participants will vary depending on the specific situation.

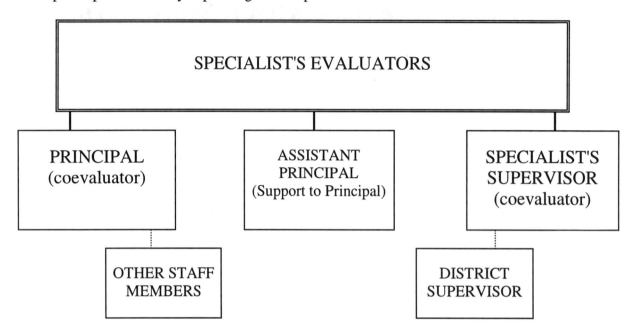

The role of the evaluators should be clarified early in the process. The following role descriptions serve as a guide, but will depend on practices and procedures in individual districts:

Principal - The principal is the primary evaluator. In this role, he or she coordinates the evaluation process, issues letters relative to the evaluation process, maintains the documentation, and is the main presenter at the unsatisfactory evaluation conferences/hearings.

Assistant Principal - If an assistant principal is available, he or she can make informal observations and provide assistance to supplement the assistance provided by the principal and the specialist's supervisor.

Specialist's Supervisor - Because the specialist's supervisor has expertise in the specialist's area of certification, he or she serves as a coevaluator and works closely with the principal during the evaluation process.

Other Staff Members - The "buddy" staff member and other specialists who provide assistance to the specialist being evaluated are usually not allowed by the bargaining unit/association to provide evaluative statements about the specialist or testify at unsatisfactory evaluation hearings. However, statements relative to dates, times, and the extent to which assistance was provided would be appropriate and admissible.

District Supervisor - In cases where intensive assistance plans are a part of the district's evaluation procedures, a district-level supervisor such as the Director of Curriculum may be involved in the specialist's evaluation.

The calendar on the following pages provides a general outline of the actions that should be taken by the principal, the specialist's supervisor, and an assistant principal (if there is one). The principal and the specialist's supervisor are the key evaluators and coordinate the activities of other district staff members involved in the process.

AUGUST

TASKS TO BE PERFORMED BY THE SPECIALIST'S EVALUATORS

WEEK	PRINCIPAL	ASSISTANT PRINCIPAL	SUPERVISOR
1			
2	☐ Send a welcome letter to all staff members assigned to the building. (2.2) ☐ Assign a "buddy" staff member to each new staff member and identify the "buddy" staff member in the new staff member's welcome letter. (2.3) ☐ Review contractual language, district policies, and state statutes regarding staff evaluation and dismissal.	☐ Provide orientation for "buddy" staff members assigned to assist new staff members. ☐ Review contractual language, district policies, and state statutes regarding staff evaluation and dismissal.	☐ Attend/participate in orientation sessions for new staff members. ☐ Provide assistance, plus any necessary orientation to individual specialists. ☐ Review contractual language, district policies, and state statutes regarding staff evaluation and dismissal.
3	☐ Provide orientation for all new staff members. ☐ Provide orientation for all staff members highlighting philosophy, goals, expectations, and procedures (school/staff handbook). ☐ Meet with the specialists' supervisors to develop consistent evaluation procedures and to clarify roles. ☐ Review just cause questions.	☐ Meet with the principal and specialists' supervisors to develop consistent evaluation procedures and to clarify roles. ☐ Review just cause questions.	☐ Meet with the principal and assistant principal to develop consistent evaluation procedures and to clarify roles. ☐ Review just cause questions.
4	☐ Meet with specialists and the specialists' supervisors and to discuss roles and responsibilities.	☐ Conduct informal observations and provide information to the principal. (3.2)	☐ Meet with specialists and the principal and to discuss roles and responsibilities.

SEPTEMBER

TASKS TO BE PERFORMED BY THE SPECIALIST'S EVALUATORS

WEEK	PRINCIPAL	ASSISTANT PRINCIPAL	SUPERVISOR
1	☐ Provide a written explanation of the evaluation process with samples of evaluation instruments that will be used to evaluate the specialists. (3.1, 3.2, 3.3, 3.4) ☐ Begin informal observations and continue conducting observations throughout the month. (3.2) ☐ Maintain the summary of informal observations. (3.5) ☐ Prepare individual staff files for parent complaints, samples of documents and letters prepared by the specialists, notes from the specialist regarding problems, letters from the staff to parents, and other data. ☐ Collect samples of documents and letters the specialist prepares and keep them in individual teacher files.	☐ Continue conducting informal observations and provide information to the principal. (3.2)	☐ Begin informal observations ☐ Develop an observation file. ☐ Collect samples of the specialist's work, if possible. ☐ Maintain letters or notes from the specialist.
2	☐ Prepare individualized letters to specialists identifying the principal and the supervisor as co-evaluators and a roster for specialists to initial showing receipt of the letter. (3.6) ☐ Hand deliver the evaluator identification letter to each specialist and have specialists initial receipt of their letters. (3.7) ☐ As they occur, inform the specialist about parent complaints and maintain them in a file. (3.8)	☐ Continue conducting informal observations and provide information to the principal. (3.2)	☐ Sign the evaluator identification letter or have your name listed as the coevaluator of the specialist. ☐ Discuss parental complaints with the specialist.
3	☐ Meet with the specialist's supervisor and assistant principal about evaluation plans. ☐ Conduct informal observations. (3.2)	☐ Continue conducting informal observations and provide information to the principal. (3.2) ☐ Meet with principal and specialist's supervisor about evaluation plans	☐ Meet with assistant principal and specialist's supervisor about evaluation plans. ☐ Conduct informal observations. (3.2)

| 4 | ☐ Hold group meetings for all specialists throughout the month.
☐ Hold planning conferences with individual specialists and the specialist's supervisor.
☐ If the quality of work samples and/or interpersonal interactions of the specialist are poor, meet with the specialist and offer suggestions for improvement.
☐ If the quality of work samples and/or interpersonal interactions of the specialist are poor, meet with the specialist and offer suggestions for improvement. | ☐ Continue conducting informal observations and provide information to the principal. (3.2) | ☐ Hold planning conferences with individual specialists and the principal.
☐ Conduct informal observations. (3.2)
☐ Offer the specialist suggestions for improvement that are consistent with those from the principal. |

OCTOBER

TASKS TO BE PERFORMED BY THE SPECIALIST'S EVALUATORS

WEEK	PRINCIPAL	ASSISTANT PRINCIPAL	SUPERVISOR
1	☐ Continue conducting daily informal observations of all staff members and record on the summary chart. (3.2 and 3.5) ☐ Meet with the specialist's supervisor and assistant principal to discuss concerns about particular specialists. ☐ Conduct formal observations, provide feedback listing areas of weakness and recommendations for improvement, and give a reasonable amount of time for improvement. (3.4 and 4.1) ☐ Following the observation, write a memorandum of concerns listing suggestions for improvement and hold a meeting to discuss the concerns. (4.1) ☐ Meet with the specialist and specialist's supervisor to discuss observations, concerns, and assistance. ☐ Provide an opportunity for the specialist to observe specialist in the same school. (4.2) ☐ Continue collecting items for individual staff files including parent complaints and work samples.	☐ Continue conducting informal observations and provide information to the principal. (3.2) ☐ Meet with the principal and supervisor to discuss concerns about particular specialists.	☐ Meet with the principal and assistant principal to discuss concerns about particular specialists. ☐ Conduct formal observations. (3.3) ☐ Meet with the specialist and principal to discuss observations, concerns, and assistance.
2	☐ Provide an opportunity for the specialist to shadow a successful specialist in another school for the entire day. (4.3) ☐ Continue to conduct formal observations, provide feedback listing areas of weakness and recommendations for improvement, and give a reasonable amount of time for improvement. (3.4 and 4.9) ☐ Meet with the specialist's supervisor to discuss concerns and support given to the specialist.	☐ Continue conducting informal observations and provide information to the principal. (3.2)	☐ Meet with the specialist before he/she visits a specialist in another school to clarify the purpose of the visit. ☐ Meet with the principal to discuss concerns and support given to the specialist.

| 3 | ☐ Provide an opportunity for a specialist from another school to work for a day with the specialist. (4.4)
☐ Offer the specialist articles to read. (4.5)
☐ Refer the specialist to appropriate sections in the school/staff handbook. (4.6)
☐ Provide opportunities for the specialist to attend workshops conducted by the school district. (4.7)
☐ Examine conference and convention guides to identify workshops to recommend for the specialist to attend. (4.8)
☐ Continue to conduct formal observations, provide feedback listing areas of weakness and recommendations for improvement, and give a reasonable amount of time for improvement. (3.4 and 4.9) | ☐ Continue conducting informal observations and provide information to the principal. (3.2) | ☐ Select articles for the specialist to read.
☐ Work with the principal to identify workshops for the specialist to attend.
☐ Meet with the specialist after he/she has visited a specialist in another school and summarize the conference.
☐ Write a summary letter about the support offered to the specialist. (4.10) |
| 4 | ☐ Write a memorandum to the district office requesting observation of and assistance for the specialist. (4.11)
☐ If the specialist does not improve, issue a letter summarizing the post-observation conference. Send a potential unsatisfactory evaluation update letter to your supervisor. (4.12)
☐ Issue a memorandum of accomplishment of recommendations. (4.13)
☐ Prepare an unsatisfactory evaluation binder with a cover page, table of contents, and a divider for each section. (4.14 and 4.15)
☐ If the specialist is improving, note the fact on the evaluation form, but re-emphasize the suggestions for improvement.
☐ Check pertinent historical information about the specialist's background in the school district. (4.16)
☐ Meet with the specialist's supervisor and assistant principal to discuss concerns about the specialist. | ☐ Continue conducting informal observations and provide information to the principal. (3.2)
☐ Meet with the principal and supervisor to discuss concerns about the specialist. | ☐ Meet with the principal and assistant principal to discuss progress and continued need for improvement.
☐ Continue to provide support and assistance to the specialist. |

TASKS TO BE PERFORMED BY THE SPECIALIST'S EVALUATORS

WEEK	PRINCIPAL	ASSISTANT PRINCIPAL	SUPERVISOR
1	❑ Continue conducting daily informal observations of all staff members and record on the summary chart. (3.2 and 3.5) ❑ Continue collecting items for individual staff member's files. ❑ Provide opportunities for the specialist to attend workshops conducted by the school district. (4.7) ❑ Send a letter to the specialist reviewing assistance provided. (4.10)	❑ Continue conducting informal observations and provide information to the principal. (3.2) ❑ Offer suggestions to the principal about recommendations for the specialist.	❑ Continue conducting observations. ❑ Work with the principal to develop letter to the specialist about assistance provided.
2	❑ Offer the specialist articles with suggestions for improvement. (4.5) ❑ Continue conduct formal observations, provide feedback listing areas of weakness and recommendations for improvement, and give a reasonable amount of time for improvement. (3.4 and 4.9) ❑ Following the observation, write a memorandum of concerns listing suggestions for improvement and hold a meeting to discuss the concerns. (4.1) ❑ Meet with the specialist's supervisor and assistant principal to discuss progress and continued need for improvement.	❑ Continue conducting informal observations and provide information to the principal. (3.2)	❑ Meet with the principal and assistant principal to discuss progress and continued need for improvement.
3	❑ Send a potential unsatisfactory evaluation update letter to your supervisor. (4.12) ❑ Maintain contact with the district's personnel department representative and attorney.	❑ Continue conducting informal observations and provide information to the principal. (3.2)	❑ Continue conducting observations. (3.4)
4	❑ Continue to conduct formal observations, provide feedback listing areas of weakness and recommendations for improvement, and give a reasonable amount of time for improvement. (3.4 and 4.9)	❑ Continue conducting informal observations and provide information to the principal. (3.2)	❑ Continue conducting observations. (3.4)

DECEMBER

TASKS TO BE PERFORMED BY THE SPECIALIST'S EVALUATORS

WEEK	PRINCIPAL	ASSISTANT PRINCIPAL	SUPERVISOR
1	☐ Continue conducting daily informal observations of all staff members and record on the summary chart. (3.2 and 3.5) ☐ Continue collecting items for individual staff member's files. ☐ Following the observation, write a memorandum of concerns listing suggestions for improvement and hold a meeting to discuss the concerns. (4.1) ☐ Meet with the specialist's supervisor and assistant principal to discuss progress and continued need for improvement.	☐ Continue conducting informal observations and provide information to the principal. (3.2) ☐ Meet with the principal and specialist's supervisor to discuss progress and continued need for improvement.	☐ Meet with the principal and assistant principal to discuss progress and continued need for improvement.
2	☐ Provide the specialist articles on needed areas of improvement. (4.5) ☐ Continue collecting items for individual specialist's files. ☐ Continue to conduct formal observations, provide feedback listing areas of weakness and recommendations for improvement, and give a reasonable amount of time for improvement. (3.4 and 4.9) ☐ Send a potential unsatisfactory evaluation update letter to your supervisor. (4.12) ☐ Provide opportunities for the specialist to attend workshops conducted by the school district. (4.7)	☐ Continue conducting informal observations and provide information to the principal. (3.2)	☐ Meet with the principal to develop the potential unsatisfactory evaluation letter. (5.3) ☐ Continue conducting formal observations. (3.4)
3	☐ Maintain contact with the district's personnel department representative and attorney. ☐ Implement a formalized intensive assistance plan if it is required in your district. (5.1 and 5.2) ☐ Issue the letter stating the possibility of issuing an unsatisfactory evaluation if the specialist's performance does not improve. (5.3)	☐ Continue conducting informal observations and provide information to the principal. (3.2)	
4	☐ Continue conducting daily observations of all staff members	☐ Continue conducting informal observations and provide information to the principal. (3.2)	

JANUARY

TASKS TO BE PERFORMED BY THE SPECIALIST'S EVALUATORS

WEEK	PRINCIPAL	ASSISTANT PRINCIPAL	SUPERVISOR
1	☐ Continue conducting daily informal observations of all staff members and record on the summary chart. (3.2 and 3.5) ☐ Continue collecting items for individual staff member's files. ☐ Maintain contact with the district's personnel department representative and attorney.	☐ Continue conducting informal observations and provide information to the principal. (3.2)	☐ Continue conducting formal observations. (3.4)
2	☐ Issue the letter stating the intent to issue an unsatisfactory evaluation in the afternoon and send a copy to the specialist's bargaining unit. (7.1) ☐ Prepare the opening and closing statements for the unsatisfactory evaluation conference proceedings. (7.2 and 7.3) ☐ Review the unsatisfactory evaluation binder to ensure that all appropriate documentation is included. ☐ Meet with your supervisor to discuss the unsatisfactory evaluation documentation and write the unsatisfactory evaluation using your district's established form and letter of transmittal. (7.5 and 7.6) ☐ Prepare copies of the unsatisfactory evaluation binder (1 for the specialist's representative, 1 for the school district representative, 1 for the supervisor, and 1 for the principal). ☐ Continue to conduct formal observations, provide feedback listing areas of weakness and recommendations for improvement, and give a reasonable amount of time for improvement. (3.4 and 4.9)	☐ Continue conducting informal observations and provide information to the principal. (3.2)	☐ Meet with the principal to assist in the preparation of the opening and closing statements and to review documentation. ☐ Meet with the specialist to discuss the unsatisfactory evaluation and letter. (7.5 and 7.6)
3	☐ Meet with the specialist's supervisor and assistant principal to discuss the unsatisfactory evaluation documentation and finalize plans for the school-level conference.	☐ Continue conducting informal observations and provide information to the principal. (3.2) ☐ Meet with the principal and specialist's supervisor to finalize plans for the school-level conference.	☐ Meet with the principal and assistant principal to finalize plans for the school-level conference.

| 4 | ☐ Send a letter reminding the specialist about the unsatisfactory evaluation conference. (7.4)

☐ Prepare for the conference and cross-examination, including seating arrangements, greeting, and guidelines. Be prepared for questions that might be asked by the specialist's legal advisor. (7.7 and 7.8)

☐ Conduct the school-level unsatisfactory evaluation conference.

☐ Send the unsatisfactory evaluation form to the district's personnel department (7.5 and 7.6). | ☐ Attend the school-level unsatisfactory evaluation conference to take notes. | ☐ Attend and participate in the school-level unsatisfactory evaluation conference. |

FEBRUARY

TASKS TO BE PERFORMED BY THE SPECIALIST'S EVALUATORS

WEEK	PRINCIPAL	ASSISTANT PRINCIPAL	SUPERVISOR
1	☐ Continue conducting daily informal observations of all staff members and record on the summary chart. (3.2 and 3.5) ☐ Continue collecting items for individual staff member's files. ☐ Prepare for presenting the unsatisfactory documentation at the next level(s). ☐ Meet with the specialist's supervisor to discuss preparation for the district-level unsatisfactory hearing.	☐ Continue conducting informal observations and provide information to the principal. (3.2)	☐ Meet with the principal to discuss preparation for the district-level unsatisfactory hearing.
2	☐ Continue to conduct formal observations, provide feedback listing areas of weakness and recommendations for improvement, and give a reasonable amount of time for improvement. (3.4 and 4.9) ☐ Maintain contact with the district's personnel department representative and attorney.	☐ Continue conducting informal observations and provide information to the principal. (3.2)	☐ Continue conducting formal observations. (3.4)
3	☐ Continue conducting formal and informal observations. (3.2 and 3.4)	☐ Continue conducting informal observations and provide information to the principal. (3.2)	
4	☐ Continue conducting formal and informal observations. (3.2 and 3.4)	☐ Continue conducting informal observations and provide information to the principal. (3.2)	☐ Continue conducting formal observations. (3.4)

MARCH

TASKS TO BE PERFORMED BY THE SPECIALIST'S EVALUATORS

WEEK	PRINCIPAL	ASSISTANT PRINCIPAL	SUPERVISOR
1	☐ Continue conducting daily informal observations of all staff members and record on the summary chart. (3.2 and 3.5) ☐ Continue collecting items for individual staff member's files. ☐ Continue preparing evaluations for all other staff members.	☐ Continue conducting informal observations and provide information to the principal. (3.2)	☐ Continue conducting formal observations. (3.4)
2	☐ Continue to conduct formal observations, provide feedback listing areas of weakness and recommendations for improvement, and give a reasonable amount of time for improvement. (3.4 and 4.9) ☐ Maintain contact with the district's personnel department representative and attorney.	☐ Continue conducting informal observations and provide information to the principal. (3.2)	☐ Continue conducting formal observations. (3.4)
3	☐ Continue conducting formal and informal observations. (3.2 and 3.4)	☐ Continue conducting informal observations and provide information to the principal. (3.2)	☐ Continue conducting formal observations. (3.4)
4	☐ Continue conducting formal and informal observations. (3.2 and 3.4)	☐ Continue conducting informal observations and provide information to the principal. (3.2)	☐ Continue conducting formal observations. (3.4)

APRIL

TASKS TO BE PERFORMED BY THE SPECIALIST'S EVALUATORS

WEEK	PRINCIPAL	ASSISTANT PRINCIPAL	SUPERVISOR
1	☐ Continue conducting daily informal observations of all staff members and record on the summary chart. (3.2 and 3.5) ☐ Continue collecting items for individual staff member's files. ☐ Continue preparing evaluations for all other staff members.	☐ Continue conducting informal observations and provide information to the principal. (3.2)	☐ Meet with the principal to prepare for closing the school year.
2	☐ Continue conducting formal and informal observations. (3.2 and 3.4) ☐ Maintain contact with the district's personnel department representative and attorney.	☐ Continue conducting informal observations and provide information to the principal. (3.2)	☐ Continue conducting formal observations. (3.4)
3	☐ Continue conducting formal and informal observations. (3.2 and 3.4) ☐ Finalize staff evaluation documentation.	☐ Continue conducting informal observations and provide information to the principal. (3.2)	☐ Finalize evaluations documentation of specialists.
4	☐ Continue conducting formal and informal observations. (3.2 and 3.4)	☐ Continue conducting informal observations and provide information to the principal. (3.2)	☐ Continue to conduct observations.

MAY

TASKS TO BE PERFORMED BY THE SPECIALIST'S EVALUATORS

WEEK	PRINCIPAL	ASSISTANT PRINCIPAL	SUPERVISOR
1	☐ Continue conducting daily informal observations of all staff members and record on the summary chart. (3.2 and 3.5) ☐ Continue collecting items for individual staff member's files. ☐ Follow your district's timeline and procedures for issuing evaluations to other staff members. ☐ Meet with the specialist's supervisor to finalize other co-evaluations.	☐ Continue conducting informal observations and provide information to the principal. (3.2)	☐ Meet with the principal to finalize other coevaluations.
2	☐ Continue conducting formal and informal observations. (3.2 and 3.4) ☐ Meet individually with staff members requesting further clarification of their strengths and recommendations for improvement.	☐ Continue conducting informal observations and provide information to the principal. (3.2)	
3	☐ Continue conducting formal and informal observations. (3.2 and 3.4) ☐ Complete staff evaluation conferences. ☐ Review the evaluation process and modify procedures and materials as needed for the next school year.	☐ Continue conducting informal observations and provide information to the principal. (3.2)	☐ Complete coevaluations.
4	☐ Issue the closing school bulletin. ☐ Continue conducting formal and informal observations. (3.2 and 3.4) ☐ Send letters to the "buddy" staff members thanking them for providing support to new staff members. (8.10) ☐ Periodically highlight points in the closing bulletin.	☐ Continue conducting informal observations and provide information to the principal. (3.2)	

JUNE

TASKS TO BE PERFORMED BY THE SPECIALIST'S EVALUATORS

WEEK	PRINCIPAL	ASSISTANT PRINCIPAL	SUPERVISOR
1	☐ Continue conducting daily informal observations of all staff members and record on the summary chart. (3.2 and 3.5) ☐ Continue collecting items for individual staff member's files.	☐ Continue conducting informal observations and provide information to the principal. (3.2)	
2	☐ End the evaluation process.	☐ End informal observations.	☐ End the coevaluation process.
3			
4			

Resource B:
Sample Unsatisfactory
Specialist Evaluation Binder

The following sample unsatisfactory specialist evaluation documentation is provided to show the proposed organizational structure of the binder that you, as the principal and specialist's supervisor, must prepare to present the various forms and letters that substantiate the recommendation for dismissal. You may choose to modify the sequence of the sections or even some items within a section depending on your personal preference. Remember, however, that the documentation must be organized in such a way that it is easy for you to present and for the hearing officer to follow.

A sample opening statement and a sample closing statement are also provided for your reference. These statements are your personal notes and should not be given to the specialist or the specialist's representative.

Any similarity to actual persons is purely coincidental.

CRESCENT RIDGE SCHOOL DISTRICT

Kennedy Elementary School
1584 South Pineview Drive
Crescent Ridge, CA 70799
(916) 444-4444/FAX 444-4445

OPENING STATEMENT

Children with special needs must have our most effective staff members working with them. Parents of children who have the difficult responsibility of raising a special needs child do not need the additional disappointment of learning that a staff member working with their child is incompetent. It is not fair to the children and their parents to have incompetent staff members working with children, especially these children. As the school administrator, I am empowered by state statutes, board policy, and contractual agreement to evaluate specialists as well as other staff members. In order to have effective staff members working with pupils, especially children with special needs, I have a duty to observe and evaluate all staff members.

In addition to myself, the evaluators for Mr. Stevenson consisted of the supervisor, the director of instruction, and the assistant principal. We observed Mr. Stevenson on numerous occasions, and our evaluations of his performance conclude that he is incompetent and should be recommended for dismissal from the school district. My recommendation for dismissal is not based on trivial issues; rather, it is based on firsthand observations that support the following seven charges of incompetence:

1. Failure to communicate effectively with parents,

2. Failure to complete mandated reports when due,

3. Failure to maintain a harmonious and effective working relationship with parents, students, teachers, and administrators,

4. Lack of knowledge required to perform the functions of a guidance counselor,

5. Lack of self-direction, and

6. Failure to complete Individualized Educational Plans for special needs children.

(NOTE: This statement should not be included in the Unsatisfactory Evaluation Binder. These are your personal notes. It should be read at the beginning of the school level meeting and at all subsequent hearings.)

Prior to issuance of the unsatisfactory evaluation, contractual procedures were followed to ensure that procedural and substantive due process are applied. Part II (Paragraph E), on page 36 of the master contract for guidance counselors, identifies the steps that are required by the Crescent Ridge School District.

Since the beginning of the 00XX-00XX school year, Mr. Arnold Stevenson has been a guidance counselor in the Crescent Ridge School District and has worked at King Elementary and Springdale Elementary Schools. He was evaluated by the principals in those schools - Ms. Adele Simons during the 00XX-00XX school year, and by Mr. Victor Harris, Jr. during the 00XX-00XX school year. In addition, Mr. Stevenson was also observed by Ms. Marlene Harworth, guidance supervisor, during these evaluation periods. The principals and supervisor found Mr. Stevenson's performance as a guidance counselor to be below average. During those assignments in different schools, he was unable to obtain and maintain a level of acceptable performance as a guidance counselor.

Mr. Stevenson is licensed in elementary education and holds certification to work in the capacity of a counselor for grades K through 6.

The following letters regarding his/her unsatisfactory performance as a guidance counselor are on file in the personnel department:

Date	Principal	Summary of Statements Regarding Performance
12/15/XX	Ms. Adele Simons	. . . . . .
3/18/XX	Ms. Adele Simons	. . . . . .

In addition, an evaluation which warned Mr. Stevenson about his marginal performance is in his employee file in the personnel department:

Date	Principal	Summary of Statements Regarding Performance
5/23/XX	Mr. Victor Harris, Jr.	. . . . . .

Listed below is a summary of Mr. Arnold Stevenson's absenteeism during the past three school years:

Year	Number of Day Absent	Percent of Time Absent Per School Year
00XX-00XX	41 days	23%
00XX-00XX	45 days	25%
00XX-00XX (To Current Year)	20 days	22%

On two different occasions, Mr. Stevenson filed for workers' compensation related to his performance of his job:

Year	Claim	Disposition
00XX-00XX	Back injury caused by an attempt to break up a student fight	Not approved
00XX-00XX	Stress caused by numerous observations by the evaluators	Not approved

During Mr. Stevenson's assignment at Kennedy Elementary School this year, he has

- been absent for a total of 168 hours:

Date	Number of Hours	Reason
9/11-9/15/XX	40	Illness
9/21/XX	8	Court appearance
9/22-9/29/XX	40	Illness
10/16-10/20/XX	40	Illness
10/30/XX	8	Illness
11/16/XX	8	Family emergency
12/10/XX	8	Illness
12/11/XX	8	Illness
1/8/XX	8	Illness

- been late to work nine times for a total of 5.7 hours

Date	Number of Hours	Reason
9/8/XX	.5	Car trouble
9/19/XX	.5	Overslept
10/15/XX	.5	Overslept
10/25/XX	.5	Traffic on expressway
11/2/XX	1.5	Personal errand
11/3/XX	.1	Flat tire
11/23/XX	.1	Overslept
12/7/XX	1.5	Car trouble
1/13/XX	.5	Could not find car keys

- been charged with the following actions of misconduct related to the performance of his counseling duties:

Date	Charge	Disposition
10/5/XX	Leaving students unsupervised during a testing session.	Verbal warning
10/20/XX	Using undue force to detain a student.	Written reprimand
11/4/XX	Failing to inform a student's parents about a staffing conference.	Letter in file
12/3/XX	Discussing confidential information about a student with another student's parents.	Three-day suspension without pay

Parents have called me on several occasions and have written letters expressing their concerns about the services provided by Mr. Stevenson.

As we proceed, I want to emphasize that contractual procedures and due process have been followed.

- The evaluation process was consistently applied. I informed all staff members about district and school expectations. In addition, the district-approved evaluation was made known to all staff members at Kennedy Elementary School. Mr. Stevenson was not singled out, and the same standards were applied to all specialists.

- The guidance supervisor, the director of Curriculum and Instruction, the assistant principal at Kennedy Elementary School, and I conducted observations of Mr. Stevenson's job performance. These observations included all phases of his assignments as a guidance counselor.

- A continuous and accurately dated file of all observations and evaluations was maintained.

- Mr. Stevenson received written memoranda of concerns that specifying the exact nature of his performance limitations.

- In each written memorandum of concern, Mr. Stevenson received specific recommendations for correcting these deficiencies and how to achieve a satisfactory level of performance.

- Mr. Stevenson was given a reasonable period of time to make necessary improvements.

- Mr. Stevenson was informed that failure to achieve and maintain an acceptable level of performance by January 14, 00XX, would result in the issuance of an unsatisfactory evaluation.

Despite the opportunities that were provided for Mr. Stevenson to improve prior to the issuance of this unsatisfactory evaluation, he failed to achieve and maintain an acceptable level of job performance.

At this point, I will review the documentation to support issuance of this unsatisfactory evaluation.

CRESCENT RIDGE SCHOOL DISTRICT   **Kennedy Elementary School**
1584 South Pineview Drive
Crescent Ridge, CA 70799
(916) 444-4444/FAX 444-4445

CLOSING STATEMENT

Unfortunately, Mr. Stevenson's overall performance as a guidance counselor has resulted in ineffective services provided to students, especially special needs students. His failure to respond to the efforts that were made to help improve his counseling performance and his failure to _____ are justifications for issuing an unsatisfactory evaluation.

Therefore I am recommending that Mr. Arnold Stevenson be relieved of his counseling responsibilities at Kennedy Elementary School and that he be dismissed from the Crescent Ridge School District.

(NOTE: This statement should not be included in the Unsatisfactory Evaluation Binder. These are your personal notes. It should be read at the end of the school level meeting and at all subsequent hearings.)

SAMPLE

UNSATISFACTORY EVALUATION DOCUMENTATION
FOR

MR. ARNOLD STEVENSON, GUIDANCE COUNSELOR

SUBMITTED BY

DR. D. REGINA WALLS, PRINCIPAL

KENNEDY ELEMENTARY SCHOOL
CRESCENT RIDGE SCHOOL DISTRICT

JANUARY 24, 00XX

CONTENTS

CRESCENT RIDGE SCHOOL DISTRICT

Kennedy Elementary School
1584 South Pineview Drive
Crescent Ridge, CA 70799
(916) 444-4444/FAX 444-4445

SECTION I. BEGINNING OF SCHOOL LETTERS TO STAFF MEMBERS

Documents in this section include:

A. Welcome Staff at the Beginning of the School Year

B. Assigning a Buddy Staff Member

CRESCENT RIDGE SCHOOL DISTRICT

Kennedy Elementary School
1584 South Pineview Drive
Crescent Ridge, CA 70799
(916) 444-4444/FAX 444-4445

August 8, 00XX

Dear Staff:

I hope you are having a restful and pleasant summer vacation. The 00XX-00XX school year will present new challenges to all of us -- new students, new staff members, new courses, and new technology such as Internet accessibility which will be a incorporated into classroom instruction.

This school year will provide an opportunity for us to develop innovative techniques and strategies as well as implement creative ideas to serve all of our children. As always, we must continue to work together to make our Kennedy Elementary School the best school in the Crescent Ridge School District.

With much enthusiasm, I look forward to working with you this school year and meeting the challenges that lie ahead as we prepare our students to be productive citizens far into the 21st century.

Again, welcome back! This will be the best year ever at Kennedy Elementary School.

Sincerely,

D. Regina Walls, Ph.D.
Principal

CRESCENT RIDGE SCHOOL DISTRICT

Kennedy Elementary School
1584 South Pineview Drive
Crescent Ridge, CA 70799
(916) 444-4444/FAX 444-4445

August 8, 00XX

Mr. Arnold Stevenson
721 East Lyon Street
Crescent Ridge, California 70799

Dear Mr. Stevenson:

I want to extend a warm and special welcome to Kennedy Elementary School. I want to make this an educationally rewarding and successful school year for you. This will be the best year ever for students and staff at Kennedy Elementary School.

As you know, the beginning of the school year is a busy time for all of us. To help you adjust to your new school, I have assigned Mr. Edward Tillman to serve as your "buddy" staff member and to answer questions you may have about the school. I am also here to assist you in any way possible to make this a successful school year. Please feel free to contact me to discuss any concerns you may have as you begin your new assignment.

Again, welcome to Kennedy Elementary School. I am happy that you have joined our staff, and I look forward to working with you this year.

Sincerely,

D. Regina Walls, Ph.D.
Principal

CRESCENT RIDGE SCHOOL DISTRICT

Kennedy Elementary School
1584 South Pineview Drive
Crescent Ridge, CA 70799
(916) 444-4444/FAX 444-4445

SECTION II. IDENTIFICATION OF EVALUATORS

Documents in this section include:

A. Letter Identifying the Specialist's Evaluators

B. School Roster for Staff Members' Signatures Acknowledging
Receipt of Letter Identifying Evaluators

CRESCENT RIDGE SCHOOL DISTRICT

Kennedy Elementary School
1584 South Pineview Drive
Crescent Ridge, CA 70799
(916) 444-4444/FAX 444-4445

September 11, 00XX

Mr. Arnold Stevenson
Kennedy Elementary School

Dear Mr. Stevenson:

The primary purpose of evaluation is to improve job performance and to promote professional development. Evaluation is a cooperative process for improving and maintaining the quality of the educational program in the school district. The staff members should view the evaluation as a learning experience and as a way for both the staff member and the administrator to grow in understanding and knowledge. This is consistent with the contract between the Crescent Ridge Board of School Directors and the Crescent Ridge Education Association. The evaluation procedures for this school year will ensure that a cooperative plan is established by the staff member and his or her evaluator(s).

Section II (Paragraph A-1) of the Master Contract states that the identification of the evaluator(s) must be made known to the staff member by name and title by the third Friday in September of the school year. Accordingly, you are informed that your performance during the 00XX-00XX school year shall be coevaluated by me and Mr. Walter Ellerman, guidance supervisor, with possible collaboration with other administrative and supervisory staff assigned to Kennedy Elementary School. In the event that someone else must serve in my capacity, or in Mr. Ellerman's capacity, the evaluation will be conducted by that person.

If you have any questions about the evaluation process, please contact me.

Sincerely,

D. Regina Walls, Ph.D.
Principal

cc: Mr. Walter Ellerman, Guidance Supervisor

CRESCENT RIDGE SCHOOL DISTRICT

KENNEDY ELEMENTARY SCHOOL
WEDNESDAY, SEPTEMBER 11, 00XX

STAFF ROSTER

SIGNATURE	NAME
_____	Beck, Harry
_____	Carver, Ruth
_____	Gaszake, Louis
_____	Holdwitze, Leroy
_____	Kaspern, Maribeth
_____	Kieperta, Randy
_____	Mandell, Jackie
_____	McDowell, Pauline
_____	Musser, Michael
_____	Novake, Elizabeth
_____	Ragalinski, Markus
_____	Russ, Deborah
_____	Sealburg, Arthur
_____	Stevenson, Arnold
_____	Simmons, Bernard
_____	Tillman, Edward
_____	Turretin, Lorraine
_____	Urbanski, Maryann
_____	Valdez, Maria
_____	Washington, Sheila
_____	Wellington, Dale

*NOTE TO STAFF: Your signature verifies that you received a copy of your Evaluator Identification Letter.

CRESCENT RIDGE SCHOOL DISTRICT

Kennedy Elementary School
1584 South Pineview Drive
Crescent Ridge, CA 70799
(916) 444-4444/FAX 444-4445

SECTION III. EVALUATION PROCEDURES FOR THE SCHOOL

Documents in this section include:

A. Memorandum to Explain the Evaluation Process

B. Informal Observation Form

C. Formal Observation Form

D. Pre-Observation Form

E. School Specialist Job Description - Guidance Counselor

F. Reference from the Specialist's Contract -- Section II, Evaluation Procedures

CRESCENT RIDGE SCHOOL DISTRICT

Kennedy Elementary School
1584 South Pineview Drive
Crescent Ridge, CA 70799
(916) 444-4444/FAX 444-4445

Date: September 4, 00XX
To: Mr. Arnold Stevenson
From: D. Regina Walls, Principal
Re: Evaluation of Staff Members Serving in Specialist Positions

This memorandum explains procedures that will be used when conducting evaluations of staff members serving in specialist positions. The overall purpose of staff evaluation is to improve job performance and to promote professional growth of the staff members. To achieve these goals, part of the evaluation process will involve identifying of strengths and limitations in performance, and then providing suggestions for strengthening limitations. Specialists will be coevaluated by their principal and the specialist's supervisor. If a specialist works at one school, the principal and his or her supervisor will conduct the evaluation. If the specialist works in more than one school, the principals at both schools and the specialist's supervisor will conduct the evaluation. The following procedures will be used to evaluate specialists this year:

Step 1 Pre-Observation Communication (Formative)

Formal observations will be conducted for specialists scheduled for a mandatory evaluation. Formal evaluation may also be conducted for specialists not scheduled for an evaluation. At the beginning of the school year, the principal, specialist's supervisor, and specialist will meet to discuss job duties and responsibilities as well as talk about job expectations for the school year. At this pre-observation conference, the specialist will be provided with further clarification of the evaluation process and procedures, a copy of his or her job description, and any variation in forms that will be used at the work site. Forms that will be used include the Pre-Observation Planning Form, Informal Observation Form, and Formal Observation/Conference Summary Form.

Step 2 Self-Evaluation Component (Formative)

Because self-evaluation is a major component of the evaluation process for staff members, each specialist will conduct a self-analysis using a copy of the appropriate evaluation form. Prior to the post-observation conference, the specialist is to check the category that best describes his or her performance. The specialist's self-evaluation is designed to assist the staff member in reflecting on his or her performance. The self-evaluation form will not be placed in his or her district personnel file.

Step 3 Observation and Post-Observation Conference (Formative)

The specialist and the coevaluators will complete Part A of the evaluation form. During the first month of the school year, a post-observation conference will be held with the specialist to discuss his or her performance and compare the self-evaluation form with the evaluation forms completed by the co-evaluators. Strengths, limitations, and suggestions for improvement, if necessary, will also be discussed. Based on the number of suggestions for improvement, the coevaluators and specialist will determine a schedule for discussing progress being made in identified areas.

Step 4 Year-End Evaluation (Summative)

This is the final evaluation conference of the school year, and it will be held during April or May. After the conference, comments will be placed on the district evaluation form. The specialist will be asked to read the evaluation, check a box to indicate agreement or disagreement, and sign the form. If the specialist disagrees with the evaluation, he or she may attach a written response to the evaluation form and return the form along with any comments to the principal within three school days. The specialist's signature does not necessarily mean that he or she agrees with the evaluation, but that the process has been completed. A copy of the completed evaluation form will then be sent to the personnel department and placed in the specialist's file.

If you have any questions, please contact my secretary to make an appointment to see me.

CRESCENT RIDGE SCHOOL DISTRICT   **Kennedy Elementary School**

INFORMAL OBSERVATION FORM
(Observation time - less than 15 minutes)

Date_____ Start of Observation_____ End of Observation_____

Specialist's Name_____ Title_____

School Assignment _____ Non-Tenured _____ Tenured _____

Rating Scale
E=Excellent, S=Satisfactory, M=Marginal, U=Unsatisfactory, N/A=Not Applicable

Part A. Working Relationship With Others

	E	S	M	U	N/A
1. With students					
2. With parents					
3. With teachers					
4. With staff					
5. With administrators					
6. With supervisors					

Part B. Professional Responsibilities of a Guidance Counselor

	E	S	M	U	N/A
(Note to Evaluators: The criteria listed in this section should be consistent with the job description and district expectations:					
1.					
2.					
3.					
4.					
5.					
6.					
7.					
8.					

Part C. Strengths, Limitations, and Recommendations

    1. Specialist's Strengths:

    2. Specialist's Limitations:

    3. Recommendations for Improvement:

Observer's Signature and Title_____

CRESCENT RIDGE SCHOOL DISTRICT   **Kennedy Elementary School**

FORMAL OBSERVATION/CONFERENCE SUMMARY FORM
(Observation time - 15 minutes or more)

Part A. Basic Information

Conference Date_____   Start of Conference_____   End of Conference_____

Specialist's Name_____   Title_____

School Assignment_____   Non-tenured_____   Tenured_____

Observation Date(s) and Times_____   _____

_____   _____

Responsibilities and Duties Observed:

_____

_____

_____

_____

Rating Scale for Parts B and C

E=Excellent, S=Satisfactory, M=Marginal, U=Unsatisfactory, N/A=Not Applicable

Part B. Working Relationship With Others	Rating Scale				
	E	S	M	U	N/A
1. With students					
2. With parents					
3. With teachers					
4. With staff					
5. With administrators					
6. With supervisors					

Part C. Professional Responsibilities of a Guidance Counselor	Rating Scale				
	E	S	M	U	N/A
(Note to Evaluators: The criteria listed in this section should be consistent with the job description and district expectations:					
1.					
2.					
3.					
4.					
5.					
6.					
7.					
8.					
9.					
10.					
11.					
12.					
13.					
14.					
15.					
16.					
17.					
18.					
19.					
20.					
21.					
22.					
23.					

Part C. Professional Responsibilities of a Guidance Counselor

CONTINUED	Rating Scale				
	E	S	M	U	N/A
24.					
25.					
26.					
27.					
28.					
29.					
30.					

Part D. Strengths, Limitations, and Recommendations

1. Specialist's Strengths:

2. Specialist's Limitations:

3. Recommendations for Improvement:

Part E. Overall Assessment

    1. Evaluator(s') Comments

    2. Evaluator(s') Rating

      ☐ Excellent   ☐ Satisfactory   ☐ Marginal   ☐ Unsatisfactory

Part F. Joint Signatures

Note to Specialist: Your signature indicates that the conference has been held and that you have seen this report. If you disagree with this assessment of your job performance, you may attach a written response to this form. Return this form -- along with any response -- within three school days, and I will forward it the personnel department, where it will be placed in your file.

Specialist's Signature_____ Date_____

Supervisor's Signature_____Date_____

Principal's Signature_____ Date_____

CRESCENT RIDGE SCHOOL DISTRICT   **Kennedy Elementary School**

PRE-OBSERVATION WORKSHEET
(To be completed by the specialist for discussion with the observer prior to a scheduled observation.)

Specialist's Name _____ Title _____

Observer's Name _____ Title _____

Activity to be Observed_____

Date of Observation _____ Time _____

List the specific objectives for the activity that will be observed.

1.

2.

3.

4.

List the strategies that will be used to accomplish the objectives.

List how you will measure if the objectives are met.

List any circumstances or problems about which the observer should know.

List any special things you want the observer to monitor.

Plans for lesson/activity available for review.   ☐ Yes   ☐ No
Comments

Other comments.

Specialist's Signature _____ Date _____

Observer's Signature _____ Date _____
(Signature only implies that information has been discussed.)

CRESCENT RIDGE SCHOOL DISTRICT

JOB DESCRIPTION

TITLE: Guidance Counselor - Elementary School Focus

REPORTS TO: Principal and/or Supervisor

OBJECTIVE   To provide guidance and counseling services in a variety of settings in
OF POSITION: an effort to help students and their families overcome problems that interfere
              with learning and to assist students as they strive to become mature,
              educated, productive, and responsible citizens.

DUTIES AND RESPONSIBILITIES:

1. Provide group and individual counseling to students in an effort to enhance the
    personal growth, self-understanding, and maturity of students.

2. Work with students on an individual basis in an effort to solve personal problems
    relative to the home environment, family relations, health, and emotional adjustment.

3. Communicate with parents as needed in writing and through telephone conferences, as
    well as in face-to-face conference.

4. Maintain accurate records of counseling sessions with students and any meetings with
    their parents/guardians.

5. Provide assistance to students to help them discover and develop their special abilities
    and talents.

6. Assist in the orientation of new staff members relative to guidance issues and
    procedures.

7. Provide in-service training in guidance for teachers and student teachers in assigned
    school(s) including, but not limited to, the services offered through the division of
    student services, standardized assessment, maintenance of student records, and report
    preparation.

8. Enroll students new to the school and provide orientation for them relative to school
    policies, procedures, and the educational program.

9. Oversee the local school application process in relation to the district-wide school
    selection process.

10. Coordinate the application process (including recommendations from other staff
    members) for students participating in special opportunity programs.

11. Coordinate the after-school and weekend tutor program.

12. Coordinate the referral process for students believed to have exceptional education needs as well as students believed to have non-exceptional education needs.

13. Coordinate the standardized testing program, which includes receiving testing materials, ensuring procedures are followed, maintaining confidentiality of materials, and returning materials to the district office.

14. Provide assistance to faculty members relative to the interpretation of individual standardized test scores, composite test scores, and other pertinent data.

15. Coordinate the local School to Work Program, which includes: a) maintaining up-to-date occupational information for distribution to individual students as well as to classes studying occupations, and (b) coordinating field trips into the community.

16. Advise administrators and faculty on matters of student discipline.

17. Remain proactive by conferring regularly with staff members relative to potential problems students may be having.

18. Provide guidance to students relative to their participation in school and community activities.

19. Play a key role in interpreting the objectives of the school's educational program to students and their parents/guardians.

20. Interpret the guidance program to the community as a whole.

21. Maintain and protect the confidentiality of student records and cumulative folders.

22. Complete other related duties as assigned.

CONTRACT BETWEEN THE CRESCENT RIDGE SCHOOL DISTRICT AND THE
CRESCENT RIDGE EDUCATORS' ASSOCIATION
SECTION II - EVALUATION PROCEDURES

(NOTE TO EVALUATOR: Insert section from the specialist's master contract.)

CRESCENT RIDGE SCHOOL DISTRICT   **Kennedy Elementary School**
                                                 1584 South Pineview Drive
                                                 Crescent Ridge, CA 70799
                                                 (916) 444-4444/FAX 444-4445

            SECTION IV. Observation Documentation

Documentation in this section includes:

A. Pre-Observation Worksheets

B. Observation Forms

C. Summaries of Monthly Staff Observations

(Note to Evaluator: Organize documents in chronological order.)

CRESCENT RIDGE SCHOOL DISTRICT   **Kennedy Elementary School**

PRE-OBSERVATION WORKSHEET
(To be completed by the specialist for discussion with the observer prior to a scheduled observation.)

Specialist's Name _____ Title _____

Observer's Name _____ Title _____

Activity to be Observed_____

Date of Observation _____ Time _____

List the specific objectives for the activity that will be observed.

1.

2.

3.

4.

List the strategies that will be used to accomplish the objectives.

List how you will measure if the objectives are met.

List any circumstances or problems about which the observer should know.

List any special things you want the observer to monitor.

Plans for lesson/activity available for review.   ☐ Yes   ☐ No
Comments

Other comments.

Specialist's Signature _____ Date _____

Observer's Signature _____ Date _____
(Signature only implies that information has been discussed.)

CRESCENT RIDGE SCHOOL DISTRICT   **Kennedy Elementary School**

INFORMAL OBSERVATION FORM
(Observation time - less than 15 minutes)

Date_____ Start of Observation_____ End of Observation_____

Specialist's Name_____ Title_____

School Assignment _____ Non-Tenured _____ Tenured _____

Rating Scale
E=Excellent, S=Satisfactory, M=Marginal, U=Unsatisfactory, N/A=Not Applicable

Part A. Working Relationship With Others

	E	S	M	U	N/A
1. With students					
2. With parents					
3. With teachers					
4. With staff					
5. With administrators					
6. With supervisors					

Part B. Professional Responsibilities of a Guidance Counselor

	E	S	M	U	N/A
(Note to Evaluators: The criteria listed in this section should be consistent with the job description and district expectations:					
1.					
2.					
3.					
4.					
5.					
6.					
7.					
8.					

Part C. Strengths, Limitations, and Recommendations

    1. Specialist's Strengths:

    2. Specialist's Limitations:

    3. Recommendations for Improvement:

Observer's Signature and Title_____

CRESCENT RIDGE SCHOOL DISTRICT   **Kennedy Elementary School**

FORMAL OBSERVATION/CONFERENCE SUMMARY FORM
(Observation time - 15 minutes or more)

Part A. Basic Information

Conference Date_____ Start of Conference_____ End of Conference_____

Specialist's Name_____ Title_____

School Assignment_____ Non-tenured_____ Tenured_____

Observation Date(s) and Times_____ _____

_____ _____

Responsibilities and Duties Observed:

_____

_____

_____

_____

Rating Scale for Parts B and C

E=Excellent, S=Satisfactory, M=Marginal, U=Unsatisfactory, N/A=Not Applicable

Part B. Working Relationship With Others	Rating Scale				
	E	S	M	U	N/A
1. With students					
2. With parents					
3. With teachers					
4. With staff					
5. With administrators					
6. With supervisors					

Part C. Professional Responsibilities of a Guidance Counselor	Rating Scale				
	E	S	M	U	N/A
(Note to Evaluators: The criteria listed in this section should be consistent with the job description and district expectations:					
1.					
2.					
3.					
4.					
5.					
6.					
7.					
8.					
9.					
10.					
11.					
12.					
13.					
14.					
15.					
16.					
17.					
18.					
19.					
20.					
21.					
22.					
23.					

Part C. Professional Responsibilities of a Guidance Counselor	Rating Scale				
CONTINUED	E	S	M	U	N/A
24.					
25.					
26.					
27.					
28.					
29.					
30.					

Part D. Strengths, Limitations, and Recommendations

   1. Specialist's Strengths:

   2. Specialist's Limitations:

3. Recommendations for Improvement:

Part E. Overall Assessment

    1. Evaluator's Comments

    2. Evaluator's Rating

      ☐ Excellent   ☐ Satisfactory   ☐ Marginal   ☐ Unsatisfactory

Part F. Joint Signatures

Note to Specialist: Your signature indicates that the conference has been held and that you have seen this report. If you disagree with this assessment of your job performance, you may attach a written response to this form. Return this form -- along with any response -- within three school days, and I will forward it the personnel department, where it will be placed in your file.

Specialist's Signature_____ Date_____

Supervisor's Signature_____Date_____

Principal's Signature_____ Date_____

SUMMARY OF OBSERVATIONS OF STAFF MEMBERS
AUGUST, 00XX

SCHOOL___Kennedy Elementary_____   PRINCIPAL____D. Regina Walls___

(Insert the dates that school is in session along the top row, and write the names of all staff members in the first column. Place the initials of the administrator or supervisor in the grid to indicate that an observation was made and by whom. Circle the initials for a formal observation or use a check mark for an informal observation.)

STAFF MEMBER																								
Beck, Harry																								
Carver, Ruth																								
Gaszake, Louis																								
Holdwitze, Leroy																								
Kaspern, Maribeth																								
Keiperta, Randy																								
McDowell, Pauline																								
Mandell, Jackie																								
Musser, Michael																								
Novake, Elizabeth																								
Ragalinski, Markus																								
Russ, Deborah																								
Sealburg, Arthur																								
Stevenson, Arnold																								
Simmons, Bernard																								
Tillman, Edward																								
Turretin, Lorraine																								
Urbanski, Maryann																								
Valdez, Maria																								
Washington, Sheila																								
Wellington, Dale																								

SUMMARY OF OBSERVATIONS OF STAFF MEMBERS
SEPTEMBER, 00XX

SCHOOL___Kennedy Elementary_____   PRINCIPAL___D. Regina Walls___

(Insert the dates that school is in session along the top row, and write the names of all staff members in the first column. Place the initials of the administrator or supervisor in the grid to indicate that an observation was made and by whom. Circle the initials for a formal observation or use a check mark for an informal observation.)

STAFF MEMBER																							
Beck, Harry																							
Carver, Ruth																							
Gaszake, Louis																							
Holdwitze, Leroy																							
Kaspern, Maribeth																							
Keiperta, Randy																							
McDowell, Pauline																							
Mandell, Jackie																							
Musser, Michael																							
Novake, Elizabeth																							
Ragalinski, Markus																							
Russ, Deborah																							
Sealburg, Arthur																							
Stevenson, Arnold																							
Simmons, Bernard																							
Tillman, Edward																							
Turretin, Lorraine																							
Urbanski, Maryann																							
Valdez, Maria																							
Washington, Sheila																							
Wellington, Dale																							

SUMMARY OF OBSERVATIONS OF STAFF MEMBERS
OCTOBER, 00XX

SCHOOL___Kennedy Elementary_____   PRINCIPAL___D. Regina Walls___

(Insert the dates that school is in session along the top row, and write the names of all staff members in the first column. Place the initials of the administrator or supervisor in the grid to indicate that an observation was made and by whom. Circle the initials for a formal observation or use a check mark for an informal observation.)

STAFF MEMBER																							
Beck, Harry																							
Carver, Ruth																							
Gaszake, Louis																							
Holdwitze, Leroy																							
Kaspern, Maribeth																							
Kieperta, Randy																							
McDowell, Pauline																							
Mandell, Jackie																							
Musser, Michael																							
Novake, Elizabeth																							
Ragalinski, Markus																							
Russ, Deborah																							
Sealburg, Arthur																							
Stevenson, Arnold																							
Simmons, Bernard																							
Tillman, Edward																							
Turretin, Lorraine																							
Urbanski, Maryann																							
Valdez, Maria																							
Washington, Sheila																							
Wellington, Dale																							

SUMMARY OF OBSERVATIONS OF STAFF MEMBERS
NOVEMBER, 00XX

SCHOOL___Kennedy Elementary_____   PRINCIPAL___D. Regina Walls___

(Insert the dates that school is in session along the top row, and write the names of all staff members in the first column. Place the initials of the administrator or supervisor in the grid to indicate that an observation was made and by whom. Circle the initials for a formal observation or use a check mark for an informal observation.)

STAFF MEMBER																							
Beck, Harry																							
Carver, Ruth																							
Gaszake, Louis																							
Holdwitze, Leroy																							
Kaspern, Maribeth																							
Kieperta, Randy																							
McDowell, Pauline																							
Mandell, Jackie																							
Musser, Michael																							
Novake, Elizabeth																							
Ragalinski, Markus																							
Russ, Deborah																							
Sealburg, Arthur																							
Stevenson, Arnold																							
Simmons, Bernard																							
Tillman, Edward																							
Turretin, Lorraine																							
Urbanski, Maryann																							
Valdez, Maria																							
Washington, Sheila																							
Wellington, Dale																							

SUMMARY OF OBSERVATIONS OF STAFF MEMBERS
DECEMBER, 00XX

SCHOOL Kennedy Elementary   PRINCIPAL   D. Regina Walls

(Insert the dates that school is in session along the top row, and write the names of all staff members in the first column. Place the initials of the administrator or supervisor in the grid to indicate that an observation was made and by whom. Circle the initials for a formal observation or use a check mark for an informal observation.)

STAFF MEMBER																							
Beck, Harry																							
Carver, Ruth																							
Gaszake, Louis																							
Holdwitze, Leroy																							
Kaspern, Maribeth																							
Kieperta, Randy																							
McDowell, Pauline																							
Mandell, Jackie																							
Musser, Michael																							
Novake, Elizabeth																							
Ragalinski, Markus																							
Russ, Deborah																							
Sealburg, Arthur																							
Stevenson, Arnold																							
Simmons, Bernard																							
Tillman, Edward																							
Turretin, Lorraine																							
Urbanski, Maryann																							
Valdez, Maria																							
Washington, Sheila																							
Wellington, Dale																							

SUMMARY OF OBSERVATIONS OF STAFF MEMBERS
JANUARY, 00XX

SCHOOL   Kennedy Elementary   PRINCIPAL   D. Regina Walls

(Insert the dates that school is in session along the top row, and write the names of all staff members in the first column. Place the initials of the administrator or supervisor in the grid to indicate that an observation was made and by whom. Circle the initials for a formal observation or use a check mark for an informal observation.)

STAFF MEMBER																						
Beck, Harry																						
Carver, Ruth																						
Gaszake, Louis																						
Holdwitze, Leroy																						
Kaspern, Maribeth																						
Kieperta, Randy																						
McDowell, Pauline																						
Mandell, Jackie																						
Musser, Michael																						
Novake, Elizabeth																						
Ragalinski, Markus																						
Russ, Deborah																						
Sealburg, Arthur																						
Stevenson, Arnold																						
Simmons, Bernard																						
Tillman, Edward																						
Turretin, Lorraine																						
Urbanski, Maryann																						
Valdez, Maria																						
Washington, Sheila																						
Wellington, Dale																						

SUMMARY OF OBSERVATIONS OF STAFF MEMBERS
FEBRUARY, 00XX

SCHOOL___Kennedy Elementary_____   PRINCIPAL___D. Regina Walls___

(Insert the dates that school is in session along the top row, and write the names of all staff members in the first column. Place the initials of the administrator or supervisor in the grid to indicate that an observation was made and by whom. Circle the initials for a formal observation or use a check mark for an informal observation.)

STAFF MEMBER																							
Beck, Harry																							
Carver, Ruth																							
Gaszake, Louis																							
Holdwitze, Leroy																							
Kaspern, Maribeth																							
Kieperta, Randy																							
McDowell, Pauline																							
Mandell, Jackie																							
Musser, Michael																							
Novake, Elizabeth																							
Ragalinski, Markus																							
Russ, Deborah																							
Sealburg, Arthur																							
Stevenson, Arnold																							
Simmons, Bernard																							
Tillman, Edward																							
Turretin, Lorraine																							
Urbanski, Maryann																							
Valdez, Maria																							
Washington, Sheila																							
Wellington, Dale																							

SUMMARY OF OBSERVATIONS OF STAFF MEMBERS
MARCH, 00XX

SCHOOL___Kennedy Elementary_____   PRINCIPAL____D. Regina Walls___

(Insert the dates that school is in session along the top row, and write the names of all staff members in the first column. Place the initials of the administrator or supervisor in the grid to indicate that an observation was made and by whom. Circle the initials for a formal observation or use a check mark for an informal observation.)

STAFF MEMBER																								
Beck, Harry																								
Carver, Ruth																								
Gaszake, Louis																								
Holdwitze, Leroy																								
Kaspern, Maribeth																								
Kieperta, Randy																								
McDowell, Pauline																								
Mandell, Jackie																								
Musser, Michael																								
Novake, Elizabeth																								
Ragalinski, Markus																								
Russ, Deborah																								
Sealburg, Arthur																								
Stevenson, Arnold																								
Simmons, Bernard																								
Tillman, Edward																								
Turretin, Lorraine																								
Urbanski, Maryann																								
Valdez, Maria																								
Washington, Sheila																								
Wellington, Dale																								

SUMMARY OF OBSERVATIONS OF STAFF MEMBERS
APRIL, 00XX

SCHOOL___Kennedy Elementary_____   PRINCIPAL____D. Regina Walls___

(Insert the dates that school is in session along the top row, and write the names of all staff members in the first column. Place the initials of the administrator or supervisor in the grid to indicate that an observation was made and by whom. Circle the initials for a formal observation or use a check mark for an informal observation.)

STAFF MEMBER																						
Beck, Harry																						
Carver, Ruth																						
Gaszake, Louis																						
Holdwitze, Leroy																						
Kaspern, Maribeth																						
Kieperta, Randy																						
McDowell, Pauline																						
Mandell, Jackie																						
Musser, Michael																						
Novake, Elizabeth																						
Ragalinski, Markus																						
Russ, Deborah																						
Sealburg, Arthur																						
Stevenson, Arnold																						
Simmons, Bernard																						
Tillman, Edward																						
Turretin, Lorraine																						
Urbanski, Maryann																						
Valdez, Maria																						
Washington, Sheila																						
Wellington, Dale																						

SUMMARY OF OBSERVATIONS OF STAFF MEMBERS
MAY, 00XX

SCHOOL___Kennedy Elementary___   PRINCIPAL___D. Regina Walls___

(Insert the dates that school is in session along the top row, and write the names of all staff members in the first column. Place the initials of the administrator or supervisor in the grid to indicate that an observation was made and by whom. Circle the initials for a formal observation or use a check mark for an informal observation.)

STAFF MEMBER																							
Beck, Harry																							
Carver, Ruth																							
Gaszake, Louis																							
Holdwitze, Leroy																							
Kaspern, Maribeth																							
Kieperta, Randy																							
McDowell, Pauline																							
Mandell, Jackie																							
Musser, Michael																							
Novake, Elizabeth																							
Ragalinski, Markus																							
Russ, Deborah																							
Sealburg, Arthur																							
Stevenson, Arnold																							
Simmons, Bernard																							
Tillman, Edward																							
Turretin, Lorraine																							
Urbanski, Maryann																							
Valdez, Maria																							
Washington, Sheila																							
Wellington, Dale																							

SUMMARY OF OBSERVATIONS OF STAFF MEMBERS
JUNE, 00XX

SCHOOL___Kennedy Elementary_____   PRINCIPAL___D. Regina Walls___

(Insert the dates that school is in session along the top row, and write the names of all staff members in the first column. Place the initials of the administrator or supervisor in the grid to indicate that an observation was made and by whom. Circle the initials for a formal observation or use a check mark for an informal observation.)

STAFF MEMBER																									
Beck, Harry																									
Carver, Ruth																									
Gaszake, Louis																									
Holdwitze, Leroy																									
Kaspern, Maribeth																									
Kieperta, Randy																									
McDowell, Pauline																									
Mandell, Jackie																									
Musser, Michael																									
Novake, Elizabeth																									
Ragalinski, Markus																									
Russ, Deborah																									
Sealburg, Arthur																									
Stevenson, Arnold																									
Simmons, Bernard																									
Tillman, Edward																									
Turretin, Lorraine																									
Urbanski, Maryann																									
Valdez, Maria																									
Washington, Sheila																									
Wellington, Dale																									

SECTION V. IDENTIFIED NEED FOR IMPROVEMENT

Documents in this section include:

A. Summary Letters of Conferences Following Observations of the Specialist

B. Memoranda of Concerns and Recommendations

C. Memoranda of Accomplishments

(Note to Evaluators: Organize documents in chronological order.)

CRESCENT RIDGE SCHOOL DISTRICT

Kennedy Elementary School
1584 South Pineview Drive
Crescent Ridge, CA 70799
(916) 444-4444/FAX 444-4445

October 9, 00XX

Mr. Arnold Stevenson
Kennedy Elementary School

Dear Mr. Stevenson:

On Tuesday, October 8, 00XX, I met with you to discuss my observation of the grade level meetings that you conducted that morning for teachers to provide them with information relative to the administration of the state writing assessment to all students in grades four and six.

You started the meetings on time and provided packets of printed materials for each teacher. However, I have the following concerns about your performance:

- Pages were missing from some packets.
- Your overhead transparency was incorrect with respect to the time of testing.
- You were unclear about several changes in district procedures and left confusion among the teachers.

It is important that you thoroughly prepare for these meetings. I stand ready to assist you in improving.

Sincerely,

_____

D. Regina Walls, Ph.D.
Principal

cc: Mr. Walter Ellerman, Guidance Supervisor

CRESCENT RIDGE SCHOOL DISTRICT

Kennedy Elementary School
1584 South Pineview Drive
Crescent Ridge, CA 70799
(916) 444-4444/FAX 444-4445

Date: October 14, 00XX

To: Mr. Arnold Stevenson

From: Dr. D. Regina Walls

Re: Concerns and Recommendations for Improvement

This memorandum of concerns is to inform you about my concerns relative to your performance as a guidance counselor at Kennedy Elementary School and to provide recommendations to help you improve. They are as follows:

Concern # 1 *(State concern and give an example.)*

   Recommendations *(Be specific and concise.)*

   A.

   B.

   C.

   D.

   Comments

Concern # 2 *(State concern and give an example.)*

   Recommendations *(Be specific and concise.)*

   A.

   B.

   C.

   D.

   Comments

Concern # 3 *(State concern and give an example.)*

Recommendations *(Be specific and concise.)*

A.

B.

C.

D.

Comments

Concern # 4 *(State concern and give an example.)*

Recommendations *(Be specific and concise.)*

A.

B.

C.

D.

Comments

I stand ready to support the improvement of your performance as a specialist, but the responsibility for that improvement clearly rests with you. If you have any questions about this memorandum or if you disagree with my concerns and recommendations, you must inform me in writing no later than October, __, 00XX or you may see my secretary to schedule a meeting with me to discuss this memorandum.

CRESCENT RIDGE SCHOOL DISTRICT

Kennedy Elementary School
1584 South Pineview Drive
Crescent Ridge, CA 70799
(916) 444-4444/FAX 444-4445

November 8, 00XX

Mr. Arnold Stevenson
Kennedy Elementary School

Dear Mr. Stevenson:

This letter is a summary of our conference held in my office at 3:30 p.m. on November 7, 00XX. I began the meeting by stating my concerns about your inability to effectively perform your duties and responsibilities as a guidance counselor. My concerns are as follows:

1. The inaccurate information you provided students about the Career Day Program.

2. Your failure to return telephone calls to parents.

3. Your conferencing techniques and insensitivity to parents.

4. Your general inability to effectively work with parents, teachers, and the administrative team.

I also offered you the following immediate suggestions to improve your counseling duties and responsibilities:

1. Read weekly staff bulletins - these provide information relative to special events and changes in schedules.

2. Implement a 24-hour call-back plan to provide timely responses to parents.

3. Enroll in the district professional development in-service on conferencing skills and interpersonal relations.

I want to continue supporting your efforts to improve your performance and effectiveness.

Sincerely,

D. Regina Walls, Ph.D.
Principal

cc: Mr. Walter Ellerman, Guidance Supervisor

CRESCENT RIDGE SCHOOL DISTRICT

Kennedy Elementary School
1584 South Pineview Drive
Crescent Ridge, CA 70799
(916) 444-4444/FAX 444-4445

November 12, 00XX

Mr. Arnold Stevenson
Kennedy Elementary School

Dear Mr. Stevenson:

On Monday, November 11, 00XX, I met with you relative to the presentation you gave to parents explaining the neighborhood tutoring program.

- Even though parents had arrived prior to the 10:30 a.m. starting time, you were still in the office collecting materials for the presentation.
- There were not enough brochures to distribute.
- You were insensitive to one parent who asked about a waiver from the registration fee.

It is important that you thoroughly plan for meetings and activities that you schedule with parents. I stand ready to assist you in improving.

Sincerely,

_____

Walter Ellerman
Guidance Supervisor

cc   Dr. D. Regina Walls, Principal

CRESCENT RIDGE SCHOOL DISTRICT

Date: November 14, 00XX

To: Mr. Arnold Stevenson

From: Dr. D. Regina Walls

Re: Accomplishment of Recommendations for Improvement

A memorandum relative to your role as a guidance counselor was sent to you in a sealed envelope, marked "confidential," on October ___, 00XX. The memorandum listed my concerns and recommendations for improving your performance as a guidance counselor. The intent of the memorandum was to provide you with clear directions to improve in your performance of your duties and responsibilities.

This is a follow-up to that memorandum and is designed to assess implementation of the recommendations that were made to improve your performance. The rating scale listed below provides an indicator to measure your attainment of the recommendations.

5= Demonstrated an excellent level of accomplishment
4= Demonstrated a satisfactory level of accomplishment
3= Demonstrated a satisfactory level of accomplishment, but needs improvement
2= Demonstrated a marginal level of accomplishment and needs substantial improvement
1= Demonstrated an unsatisfactory level of accomplishment

Concern # 1

Recommendations

    Attainment
of Recommendations

A.

    _____

B.

    _____

C.

    _____

D.

    _____

Comments

Concern # 2

Recommendations

Attainment
of Recommendations

A. _____

B. _____

C. _____

D. _____

Comments

Concern # 3

Recommendations

Attainment
of Recommendations

A. _____

B. _____

C. _____

D. _____

Comments

Concern # 4

Recommendations

Attainment
of Recommendations

A. _____

B. _____

C. _____

D. _____

Comments

Although you have made some improvements, your overall performance as a guidance counselor has not improved since my first memorandum of concerns was sent to you. You have failed to successfully respond to and implement the recommendations that were made to improve your performance. Therefore, I want to clearly state that, if your performance does not improve within the next thirty school days, you will receive an unsatisfactory evaluation.

Mr. Walter Ellerman, guidance supervisor, will continue to work with you to improve your performance. In addition, Mr. Jose Gomez, assistant principal, will to continue to conduct informal observations and offer you suggestions for improvements. As always, I will continue to conduct informal and formal observations to help you to improve your performance. Our primary purpose is to ensure that our students have a quality learning environment and that you have a successful school year.

If you have any questions about this memorandum or, if you disagree with my assessment of your performance, you should inform me in writing by no later than November 17, 00XX, or see my secretary to schedule a meeting with me to discuss this memorandum. At this meeting, you may have representation of your choice.

cc: Mr. Walter Ellerman

CRESCENT RIDGE SCHOOL DISTRICT

Kennedy Elementary School
1584 South Pineview Drive
Crescent Ridge, CA 70799
(916) 444-4444/FAX 444-4445

December 10, 00XX

Mr. Arnold Stevenson
Kennedy Elementary School

Dear Mr. Stevenson:

On Friday, December 6, 00XX, I met with you to discuss observations that were conducted on December 2 (class presentation on peer mediation) and December 4 (review conference for a student in the learning disabilities program).

I began the conference, by stating that you have shown some improvement in organizing printed materials for presentations and punctuality. However, I pointed out areas that require your attention.

Class presentation:

- You were not able to respond to basic questions relative to the logistics of the peer mediation program that will be implemented next week.
- The group of students you selected to mediate next week is not representative of the student population (i.e., ethnic and gender composition)

Review conference:

- You had inaccurately informed the parent that the conference would be held at 2:00 p.m.
- You left confidential documents on a chair in the conference room and did not find them until the next day.

I stand ready to assist you in improving.

Sincerely,

_____

D. Regina Walls, Ph.D.
Principal

cc: Mr. Walter Ellerman, Guidance Supervisor

CRESCENT RIDGE SCHOOL DISTRICT

Kennedy Elementary School
1584 South Pineview Drive
Crescent Ridge, CA 70799
(916) 444-4444/FAX 444-4445

SECTION VI. LETTERS/DOCUMENTS RELATIVE TO ASSISTANCE PROVIDED

Documents in this section include:

A. Observation of a Specialist in the Same School

B. Visitation by the Specialist to Another School

C. Visitation by a Specialist From Another School

D. Section in the Staff Handbook

E. Articles to Read

F. Workshop/In-Service Opportunity to Attend

G. Convention to Attend

H. Request for Observation by a District Supervisor Related to the Intensive Assistance Plan

I. Review of Assistance

(Note to Evaluators: If your district requires a formal intensive assistance plan, it should be included in this section.)

CRESCENT RIDGE SCHOOL DISTRICT

Kennedy Elementary School
1584 South Pineview Drive
Crescent Ridge, CA 70799
(916) 444-4444/FAX 444-4445

October 2, 00XX

Mr. Arnold Stevenson
Kennedy Elementary School

Dear Mr. Stevenson:

I want you to have the opportunity to improve your job performance as a guidance counselor. As your evaluator, I am concerned about how you interact with students and teachers. I would like you to shadow Ms. Deborah Russ, Social Worker at Kennedy Elementary School, to observe how she works with students and teachers. Specific areas include:

- Interpersonal skills
- Methods for scheduling conferences and providing feedback to teachers and administrators
- Conferencing techniques

Mr. Jose Gomez will coordinate the arrangements.

Again, I am ready to assist in making this school year a successful experience for you.

Sincerely,

D. Regina Walls, Ph.D.
Principal

cc: Mr. Walter Ellerman, Guidance Supervisor
Mr. Jose Gomez, Assistant Principal

CRESCENT RIDGE SCHOOL DISTRICT

Kennedy Elementary School
1584 South Pineview Drive
Crescent Ridge, CA 70799
(916) 444-4444/FAX 444-4445

October 10, 00XX

Mr. Arnold Stevenson
Kennedy Elementary School

Dear Mr. Stevenson:

I want you to have a successful experience as the guidance counselor at Kennedy Elementary School. As we have discussed earlier, opportunities are available for you to observe at other schools in the Crescent Ridge School District. Therefore, I have made arrangements for you to spend an entire day at Sunny Drive Elementary School which is located at 4827 South Sunny Drive.

You are to report to Sunny Drive Elementary School on October 15, 00XX. You will spend the entire day working with Mr. Daniel Kirkland, guidance counselor, who has extensive experiences working with special education students. If you find this to be a worthwhile experience, I can also arrange to have Mr. Kirkland visit you here at Kennedy Elementary School.

Again, I stand ready to assist you to make this school year a successful experience.

Sincerely,

D. Regina Walls, Ph.D.
Principal

cc: Mr. Walter Ellerman, Guidance Supervisor

CRESCENT RIDGE SCHOOL DISTRICT

Kennedy Elementary School
1584 South Pineview Drive
Crescent Ridge, CA 70799
(916) 444-4444/FAX 444-4445

October 17, 00XX

Mr. Arnold Stevenson
Kennedy Elementary School

Dear Mr. Stevenson:

I was pleased that your visit to Sunny Drive Elementary School was an worthwhile professional development activity for you. I want to continue assisting you to improve your job performance. Therefore, I have made arrangements for Mr. Daniel Kirkland, guidance counselor from Sunny Drive Elementary School, to spend the entire school day with you on Monday, October 15, 00XX. During that time, Mr. Kirkland will work with you in the following areas:

- Planning and record keeping
- General organization
- Feedback provided to teachers and administrators
- Preparing student Individual Educational Plans (IEPs)
- Working with special needs children and parents

Again, I stand ready to assist you in making this school year a successful experience.

Sincerely,

D. Regina Walls, Ph.D.
Principal

cc:　Mr. Walter Ellerman, Guidance Supervisor

CRESCENT RIDGE SCHOOL DISTRICT

Kennedy Elementary School
1584 South Pineview Drive
Crescent Ridge, CA 70799
(916) 444-4444/FAX 444-4445

October 21, 00XX

Mr. Arnold Stevenson
Kennedy Elementary School

Dear Mr. Stevenson:

The Kennedy Elementary School Staff Handbook is designed to provide information relative to procedures at our school. Because you had difficulty in completing your report identifying students recommended for special services on time, multi-disciplinary team conferences for two students could not be held according to the mandated timeline. A copy of the following sections on expectations for meeting the needs of special education children are enclosed. Please carefully review these sections of the handbook to prevent this situation from occurring in the future:

TOPIC	PAGE
Procedures for Referring EEN and Non-EEN Students	5
Guidelines for Multi-disciplinary Team Conferences	10

I hope this information is helpful to you. The school district has an obligation to adhere to the timeline to ensure that the educational needs of children are met. We must follow the guidelines that have been established by law or the district may lose future funding. If you have any questions about this memorandum, please see my secretary to make an appointment to see me.

As always, I stand ready to assist you in making this a successful school year.

Sincerely,

D. Regina Walls, Ph.D.
Principal

Enclosures

cc: Mr. Walter Ellerman, Guidance Supervisor

CRESCENT RIDGE SCHOOL DISTRICT

Kennedy Elementary School
1584 South Pineview Drive
Crescent Ridge, CA 70799
(916) 444-4444/FAX 444-4445

October 23, 00XX

Mr. Arnold Stevenson
Kennedy Elementary School

Dear Mr. Stevenson:

In an effort to assist you to improve your performance as a guidance counselor, I am providing the enclosed journal articles for you to read:

- Meeting the 504 Mandates
- Time Management for School Professionals

I stand ready to assist you in making this a successful year.

Sincerely,

D. Regina Walls, Ph.D.
Principal

Enclosures

cc: Mr. Walter Ellerman, Guidance Supervisor

CRESCENT RIDGE SCHOOL DISTRICT

Kennedy Elementary School
1584 South Pineview Drive
Crescent Ridge, CA 70799
(916) 444-4444/FAX 444-4445

October 25, 00XX

Mr. Arnold Stevenson
Kennedy Elementary School

Dear Mr. Stevenson:

The *Crescent Ridge School District Staff Bulletin* lists several in-service opportunities that may be beneficial in your efforts to improve your job performance as a guidance counselor. These in-service classes appear to be related to the concerns that I specified in the memorandum of concerns dated October 17, 00XX. Therefore, I recommend that you enroll in the following classes:

COURSE TITLE	PAGE IN BULLETIN
Implementation of 504	8
Time Management	15
Inclusion	38

I sincerely hope that these classes will help you improve your performance as a guidance counselor at Kennedy Elementary School. If you wish to discuss these classes or other school issues, please call my secretary to set up a meeting with me.

Sincerely,

Mr. Walter Ellerman
Guidance Supervisor

Enclosure

cc: Dr. D. Regina Walls, Principal

CRESCENT RIDGE SCHOOL DISTRICT

Kennedy Elementary School
1584 South Pineview Drive
Crescent Ridge, CA 70799
(916) 444-4444/FAX 444-4445

Date: November 1, 00XX

To: Dr. Edward Gilmore, Curriculum and Instruction Director

From: D. Regina Walls, Principal

Re: Request for Assistance

This is a request for assistance for Mr. Arnold Stevenson, a guidance counselor at Kennedy Elementary School. Mr. Stevenson's job performance has deteriorated to the degree that I am anticipating issuing an unsatisfactory evaluation if his performance does not improve.

Mr. Stevenson is having particular difficulty in the following areas:

- Planning and record keeping
- General organization
- Feedback provided to teachers and administrators
- Preparing student Individual Educational Plans (IEPs)
- Working with special needs children and parents
- Procedures for referring EEN and Non-EEN Students
- Guidelines for Multi-disciplinary Team Conferences

Please contact me at to finalize arrangements. Thank you for your assistance.

cc: Mr. Walter Ellerman, Guidance Supervisor

CRESCENT RIDGE SCHOOL DISTRICT

Kennedy Elementary School
1584 South Pineview Drive
Crescent Ridge, CA 70799
(916) 444-4444/FAX 444-4445

November 1, 00XX

Mr. Arnold Stevenson
Kennedy Elementary School

Dear Mr. Stevenson:

The Crescent Ridge School District Education Association (CRSDEA) Convention is scheduled to be held from Thursday, November 7, 00XX to Friday, November 8, 00XX, at the Crescent Ridge Convention Center.

The convention booklet lists several workshops that may assist you in improving your performance as a guidance counselor at Kennedy Elementary School. I recommend that you attend the following workshops:

TITLE DATE		TIME	ROOM
• Maintaining Professionalism	10/25/XX	1:00 p.m.	Timberline 1
• Discussion on Changes in Guidelines Related to Education	10/16/XX	9:00 a.m.	Meadow Brook 2

I believe this convention should be professionally rewarding. As always, I stand ready to assist you in making this school year a successful experience.

Sincerely,

D. Regina Walls, Ph.D.
Principal

cc: Mr. Walter Ellerman, Guidance Supervisor

CRESCENT RIDGE SCHOOL DISTRICT

Kennedy Elementary School
1584 South Pineview Drive
Crescent Ridge, CA 70799
(916) 444-4444/FAX 444-4445

November 4, 00XX

Mr. Arnold Stevenson
Kennedy Elementary School

Dear Mr. Stevenson:

During the past four weeks, we have made recommendations to improve your job performance as a guidance counselor in the following areas:

- Responding within State and Federal Guidelines.
  - Review the 504 Guidelines recently distributed by the Department of Exceptional Education.
  - Set up a reference file for easy access when questions arise.
- Working effectively with staff members.
  - Follow your schedule and pick up students from their classes according to arrangements previously made with their teachers.
  - Attend monthly grade level meetings.
  - Respond to inquiries in a timely fashion.
- Meeting deadlines and completing reports on time.
  - Set up a tickler file to organize tasks.
  - Plan to complete reports at least two to three days before they are due.

I would like to meet with you to further discuss these suggestions for improvement as well as progress that you believe you are making to improve your performance.

As always, I stand ready to assist you in making this school year a successful experience.

Thank you.

Sincerely,

D. Regina Walls, Ph.D.   Walter Ellerman
Principal   Guidance Supervisor

CRESCENT RIDGE SCHOOL DISTRICT

Kennedy Elementary School
1584 South Pineview Drive
Crescent Ridge, CA 70799
(916) 444-4444/FAX 444-4445

SECTION VII. PARENTAL COMPLAINTS

Documentation in this section includes:

A. Letters Informing the Specialist About Parental Complaints

B. Parental Complaints Filed Against the Specialist

(Note to Evaluators: Organize these documents in chronological order.)

CRESCENT RIDGE SCHOOL DISTRICT

Kennedy Elementary School
1584 South Pineview Drive
Crescent Ridge, CA 70799
(916) 444-4444/FAX 444-4445

September 17, 00XX

Mr. Arnold Stevenson
Kennedy Elementary School

Dear Mr. Stevenson:

Section IV (Paragraph A) of the Crescent Ridge School District Contract states that, when a parental or public complaint is filed against a staff member, the individual staff member must be notified about the complaint. Consequently, I am forwarding the attached parental complaint that I received about you on September 17, 00XX.

Please call my secretary to schedule a conference by September 19, 00XX.

Sincerely,

D. Regina Walls, Ph.D.
Principal

Attachment

CRESCENT RIDGE SCHOOL DISTRICT

KENNEDY ELEMENTARY SCHOOL
PARENTAL COMPLAINT FORM

Date_____Time_____a.m./p.m.

Student_____Grade_____ID Number_____

Address_____

Person Filing Complaint_____

Relationship to Student_____

Phone Number - Home_____   Other_____

Nature of Complaint_____

_____

_____

_____

Action Requested_____

_____

Has a Previous Complaint Been Filed Yes_____   No____   Date_____

Person(s) Spoken to:

_____
                                Name/Title/Department

_____
                                Name/Title/Department
Resolution_____

_____

_____

_____

_____

Complaint Resolved   Further Action Necessary_____

_____   _____
            Signature/Title   Date

CRESCENT RIDGE SCHOOL DISTRICT

Kennedy Elementary School
1584 South Pineview Drive
Crescent Ridge, CA 70799
(916) 444-4444/FAX 444-4445

SECTION VIII. UNSATISFACTORY EVALUATION LETTERS

Documents in this section include:

A. Failure to Achieve a Satisfactory Level of Performance

B. Intent to Issue an Unsatisfactory Evaluation

C. Meeting Notice

D. Accompanying the Unsatisfactory Evaluation

E. Evaluation

CRESCENT RIDGE SCHOOL DISTRICT

Kennedy Elementary School
1584 South Pineview Drive
Crescent Ridge, CA 70799
(916) 444-4444/FAX 444-4445

December 17, 19XX

Mr. Arnold Stevenson
Kennedy Elementary School

Dear Mr. Stevenson:

From September through December of the 00XX-00XX school year, informal and formal observations were made of you as the school guidance counselor at Kennedy Elementary School. Specifically, observations were conducted on:

Day	Date	Time	Observer
Wednesday	9/8/XX	8:00-8:25 a.m.	D. Regina Walls
Friday	9/10/XX	10:20-10:30 a.m.	D. Regina Walls
Tuesday	9/14/XX	1:10-1:25 p.m.	Jose Gomez
Monday	9/20/XX	2:15-2:30 p.m.	D. Regina Walls
Wednesday	9/22/XX	2:45-3:00 p.m.	Jose Gomez
Monday	9/27/XX	8:10-8:30 a.m.	D. Regina Walls
Friday	10/1/XX	9:15-10:10 a.m.	Walter Ellerman
Wednesday	10/8/XX	8:05-9:00 a.m.	Walter Ellerman
Tuesday	10/12/XX	10:15-11:05 a.m.	D. Regina Walls
Tuesday	10/19/XX	9:10-10:20 a.m.	Walter Ellerman
Monday	11/1/XX	9:15-10:00 a.m.	D. Regina Walls
Tuesday	11/2/XX	1:15-1:25 p.m.	Jose Gomez
Thursday	11/11/XX	10:30-11:30 a.m.	Walter Ellerman
Wednesday	11/17/XX	1:30-2:30 p.m.	D. Regina Walls
Monday	11/22/XX	8:00-9:00 a.m.	Walter Ellerman
Tuesday	11/23/XX	9:00-10:00 a.m.	Walter Ellerman
Wednesday	12/1/XX	8:00-8:45 a.m.	D. Regina Walls
Tuesday	12/7/XX	10:45-11:30 a.m.	Walter Ellerman
Thursday	12/8/XX	2:45-2:55 p.m.	Jose Gomez
Friday	12/10/XX	9:20-10:15 a.m.	D. Regina Walls
Monday	12/13/XX	1:00-1:30 p.m.	Walter Ellerman
Wednesday	12/15/XX	2:00-3:00 p.m.	D. Regina Walls

These observations represent a reasonable sampling of your performance as a guidance counselor and included all aspects of your assignment, both morning and afternoon.

In addition to memoranda that were sent to you outlining concerns relative to your performance, conferences were held with you to discuss limitations, suggestions for improvement, and available assistance as well as a reasonable length of time for necessary improvement. Letters summarizing our conferences were sent to you on October 9, November 8, and December 10, 00XX.

Unfortunately your performance has not improved to a satisfactory level. Therefore, this letter serves as official notification that failure to achieve a satisfactory level of achievement by January 15, 00XX, will result in the issuance of an unsatisfactory evaluation.

Sincerely,

_____

D. Regina Walls, Ph.D.
Principal

cc:　Mr. Walter Ellerman, Guidance Supervisor

CRESCENT RIDGE SCHOOL DISTRICT

Kennedy Elementary School
1584 South Pineview Drive
Crescent Ridge, CA 70799
(916) 444-4444/FAX 444-4445

January 17, 00XX

Mr. Arnold Stevenson
721 East Lyon Street
Crescent Ridge, California 70799

Dear Mr. Stevenson:

This letter is to inform you that an unsatisfactory evaluation of your performance as a guidance counselor will be submitted to the personnel department.

A copy of your unsatisfactory evaluation will be given to you on Friday, January 24, 00XX, at 3:30 p.m. in my office. The Master Contract, Section III on pages 25-29, will govern the procedures to ensure your due process during the evaluation hearings. If you wish, you may be represented by a member of your bargaining unit or a person of your choice.

After receiving the evaluation form, you will have three school days to review my comments and respond to them in writing if you wish. A copy of your response will be attached to the unsatisfactory evaluation form before it is submitted to the personnel department with a recommendation for your dismissal from the Crescent Ridge School District.

Sincerely,

D. Regina Walls, Ph.D.
Principal

cc: Mr. Walter Ellerman, Guidance Supervisor

CRESCENT RIDGE SCHOOL DISTRICT   **Kennedy Elementary School**
                                                1584 South Pineview Drive
                                                Crescent Ridge, CA 70799
                                              (916) 444-4444/FAX 444-4445

January 22, 00XX

Mr. Arnold Stevenson
Kennedy Elementary School

Dear Mr. Stevenson:

This letter is to remind you that a conference has been scheduled in my office at 3:30 p.m. on Friday, January 24, 00XX, to discuss the issuance of an unsatisfactory evaluation to you.

If you wish, you may be represented by a bargaining unit representative or anyone of your choice.

Sincerely,

_____

D. Regina Walls, Ph.D.
Principal

cc: Mr. Walter Ellerman, Guidance Supervisor

CRESCENT RIDGE SCHOOL DISTRICT

Kennedy Elementary School
1584 South Pineview Drive
Crescent Ridge, CA 70799
(916) 444-4444/FAX 444-4445

January 24, 00XX

Mr. Arnold Stevenson
Kennedy Elementary School

Dear Mr. Stevenson:

Enclosed is your performance evaluation for the 00XX-00XX school year. If you wish to respond in writing to this evaluation, you may attach your comments and submit them along with the evaluation form within three school days. The unsatisfactory evaluation and any comments will then be filed with the personnel department.

If you wish to meet relative to your evaluation, please contact my secretary to schedule a conference. At this meeting, you are entitled to have representation of your choice.

Sincerely,

D. Regina Walls, Ph.D.

cc: Mr. Walter Ellerman, Guidance Supervisor

CRESCENT RIDGE SCHOOL DISTRICT

PERFORMANCE EVALUATION FORM

NAME_____Arnold Stevenson_____ TITLE_____Guidance Counselor_____

SCHOOL__Kennedy Elementary School_____ EVALUATION PERIOD__00XX-00XX__

(Directions to evaluators: Use the space provided to summarize your appraisal of the performance of the staff member. If necessary, additional pages may be attached.)

Arnold Stevenson is not making a satisfactory contribution to the educational program at Kennedy Elementary School. While he has exhibited some positive characteristics, he has failed to meet the standards of the profession and expectations of the district. It is recommended that he not be included in this organization for the next semester. This action is justified because of Mr. Stevenson's

1. Failure to communicate effectively with parents,

2. Failure to complete mandated reports when due,

3. Failure to maintain a harmonious and effective working relationship with parents, students, teachers, and administrators,

4. Lack of knowledge required to perform the functions of a guidance counselor,

5. Lack of self-direction, and

6. Failure to complete Individualized Education Plan for your students.

Percent of class time lost due to absences ___ Percent of class time lost due to tardiness ___

Evaluator(s) Rating ☐ Excellent ☐ Satisfactory ☐ Marginal ☐ Unsatisfactory

_____	_____	_____
Evaluator's Signature	Title	Date
_____	_____	_____
Evaluator's Signature (If co-evaluated)	Title	Date

(Directions to staff member: After reading your performance evaluation, check indicating that you agree or disagree with your evaluator(s) statements and rating. Then sign on the lines below. Your signature only means that you have read this evaluation.)

☐ Agree   ☐ Disagree

_____	_____	_____
Staff Member's Signature	Title	Date

References

Iwanicki, E. F. (1990). Teacher evaluation for school improvement. In J. Millman & L. Darling-Hammond (Eds.), *The new handbook of teacher evaluation assessing elementary and secondary school teachers* (pp. 158-170). Newbury Park, CA: Sage.

Lawrence, C. E., & Vachon, M. K. (1995). *How to handle staff misconduct: A step-by-step guide.* Thousand Oaks, CA: Corwin.

Lawrence, C. E., Vachon, M. K., Leake, D. O., & Leake, B. H. (1993). *The marginal teacher: A step-by-step guide to fair procedures for identification and dismissal.* Newbury Park, CA: Corwin.

Natriello, G. (1990). Intended and unintended consequences: Purposes and effects of teacher evaluation. In J. Millman & L. Darling-Hammond (Eds.), *The new handbook of teacher evaluation assessing elementary and secondary school teachers* (pp. 35-45). Newbury Park, CA: Sage.

Society for Human Resource Management. (1994). *Job analysis and evaluation. Module four: Compensation and benefits.* Minneapolis, MN: Author.